Between the Now and When

Being Angels While We Wait

Between the Now and When

Being Angels While We Wait

Michelle L. Martin

Copyright © 2017 by Michelle L. Martin

All rights reserved. No part of this publication may be reproduced, distributed, or transmitted in any form or by any means, including photocopying, recording, or other electronic or mechanical methods, without the prior written permission of the author, except in the case of brief quotations embodied in critical reviews and certain other noncommercial uses permitted by copyright law.

Editing: Catherine Garrett, Heather Green, Cathy Ricci and Kathryn Taylor
Design: Angie Lawrence

King James Bible used in all scriptural references.

ISBN:
ebook 9781630729325
paperback 9781630729332

Library of Congress Control Number: 2017961033

Izzard Ink Publishing Company
PO Box 522251
Salt Lake City, Utah 84152
www.izzardink.com

Acknowledgments

To my angel parents who have guided me all along the way!

To Heavenly Father and all His angels who have helped me, inspired me, whispered in my ear, and sometimes told me exactly what to write.

To Catherine Garrett, Heather Green, Cathy Ricci and Kathryn Taylor for their countless hours of kindness, love, and editing.

To Angie Lawrence for her creative brilliance, compassion, and generous time spent designing this book.

To Julia Hammond for her inspired foreword.

To Kara Arnold Applegate, Steven Sharp Nelson, and Steven Perlman for their time and encouragement.

To my wonderful friends who have contributed to the realization of this book: Kathy Robertson, Terra Taylor, Cathy Larson-Taylor, Katrina Troutman, Camille Kennard, Ken and Kendra Moss, Heather Rothey Lyon, David McCallister, Drew Johnson, Cara Baldree, Blake and Keltson Howell, and Johnathan Newbold.

This book is dedicated to my nieces and nephews.

Contents

FOREWORD
By Julia Hammond ix

CHAPTER 1
Bringing the Smile of Jesus to Others 1

CHAPTER 2
Ministering Angels Seen and Unseen 13

CHAPTER 3
Loving Our Neighbors 18

CHAPTER 4
Trust the Lord and Call Upon Angels 24

CHAPTER 5
Appreciate Liberty! 31

CHAPTER 6
Testify to Others 44

CHAPTER 7
Trials Can Be Mercies in Disguise 49

CHAPTER 8
Defy Your Limits 62

CHAPTER 9
Sling and a Stone 69

Foreword

My mother always told me that good things come to those who wait. Even with the anticipation of good things, waiting is difficult. Making that time count is vital, especially when the wait is extensive.

In *Between the Now and When*, Michelle L. Martin offers wonderful ways to focus our lives outside of ourselves, realizing greater purpose in our lives, especially when they take a different path than we had planned. She shares wonderful experiences, often personal and poignant, that remind us of the opportunities that await us when we put aside our own concerns and step forward to realize the wonders of this life that God has given us.

We journey with Michelle to the mountains of Honduras where she joins with others to bring smiles to the children of San Pedro Sula and their families. She shares tender moments with her sweet mother as she faces a premature death. The depth of her love for friends, those known and unknown, is witnessed as she shares meaningful anecdotes. We ache with her for those who struggle with challenges far beyond their control and gain a greater appreciation for what we have here in our own country. Being reminded of our responsibility, the needs that surround us, and the commitments we have made, our resolve is strengthened and we are given the impetus needed to "go about doing good." I am grateful to Michelle for her powerful example.

More than twenty years ago, I began experiencing problems with chronic pain, making it very difficult for me to even get up and face the day. Having to depend on my family and others for help was humiliating. I was angry with my situation and desperately sad about life in general. Many treatments were tried without success. Feeling defeated and unproductive, I spent days on the couch doing little more than feeling sorry for myself.

I was waiting for my life to change, waiting to feel better. For a very long time, I prayed to be healed, having faith that I would indeed be restored. My health didn't change. Eventually, I realized that I had a choice. I could choose to stay on the couch, consumed with myself, my problems, or I could get up and focus outside of myself.

As my focus changed from myself to others, my testimony and my faith strengthened. My energy increased and I felt purpose and joy in life. Just as we learn in this book, newfound determination enabled me to volunteer, to serve in demanding responsibilities at church, to spend extra time with those in need, to be a more dedicated friend, and to show gratitude to the "ministering angels" who had so generously served me. There were opportunities all around me to serve, to love, and to see the hand of God in my life. Facing my "Goliath" was no longer impossible. I have been, and continue to be, richly blessed by my Heavenly Father as I do my part. Those who read this book will find it useful and uplifting in their search for fulfillment during challenging waiting periods.

Between the Now and When—Being Angels While We Wait teaches us to refocus our lives in positive, meaningful ways, realizing that the twists and turns and experiences off the beaten path are the most precious and powerful. We were not put on this earth as observers, but as participants. There is no joy in waiting, but there is great joy in dedicating that time to our Father and His Son. Good things do indeed come to those who wait.

    Michelle is a woman of integrity who lives her life ever thoughtful of others and their needs. Her compassion and inner strength combine to make her a powerful force for good in this life. I join her in testifying that our Father in Heaven and His Son, Jesus Christ, care deeply for us and desire the greatest joy for us. May we seek and find it as we dedicate our lives to Their service.

—Julia Hammond
Mother and Friend Devoted to Christ

CHAPTER 1

Bringing the Smile of Jesus to Others

"Every time you smile at someone, it is an action of love, a gift to that person, a beautiful thing."
Mother Teresa

We are all waiting for something to happen in life. Many times, we say we will be happy when…when I graduate, when I get married, when I find a job, when I'm healthy or healed, when I can finally get pregnant and have a baby, when I get that raise or promotion at work. We are constantly waiting for something in life…waiting for someone to come home from college or overseas serving in the military, waiting to retire, waiting to feel 'normal' again after the loss of a loved one, and many more *waits* in life! One of my life-long best friends, Kathy, was recently diagnosed with leukemia. Consequently, she had to wait for a life-saving match for a bone marrow transplant. First, doctors tried her siblings—no match. Then, the national registry—no match. A few months later, they tried the international registry—finally,—a perfect match from someone on the other side of the world in Eastern Europe. While she was waiting, praying, and hoping for this miracle, we were all praying, fasting, and hoping right along with her! This book is to suggest that while we wait between the now and when, let us *be angels while we wait* and recognize the people that God has put in our path, those who help us through our own *waits*.

Three months after Kathy received her transplant, I was able to travel back to Oregon and visit with her. I was impressed with how she had *devoted this waiting period to faith in God*. She had such a strong spirit of faith about her. I knew that through this furnace of affliction, she truly had strengthened her relationship with the Savior and her Heavenly Father! I felt uplifted simply by being with her. She said to me, "I know I need to write down all these experiences so when I am better, I don't forget what the Lord has taught me."

Mortality and 'times of waiting and delay' can often cause physical pain for our hearts and souls. It is at times like these that we must dig deep, search our souls, and plead for heavenly intervention—even if it feels like no one is there! The Prince of Peace (Isaiah 9:6) will never turn His back on us. We must ask for help when we are in the thick of it, pleading and searching. He is there! Seek His counsel and guidance by calling upon ministering angels and by being an angel friend to others during your *waits!* As hard as it is to understand sometimes, I know *there is purpose in our waits.* There is comfort to be found, emotional healing to be discovered, and relief in miraculous grace. We are taught beautiful gospel truth by Thomas Moore in the Hymn *Come, Ye Disconsolate*:

> "Come, ye disconsolate, where'er ye languish;
> Come to the mercy seat, fervently kneel.
> Here bring your wounded hearts;
> here tell your anguish.
> Earth has no sorrow that heav'n cannot heal."

In my life, it is the 'waiting to be married' that can weigh heavy on my heart. But, I find that reaching outside myself, focusing on local service or humanitarian trips, helps me feel like I am dedicating this 'wait time' to God's purposes. As a licensed dental hygienist, I have enjoyed serving by going on dental/medical humanitarian trips to Central America, and one particular trip I took in November of 2014 really helped me feel like an extension of God's love.

That year, I had the privilege of joining the extraordinary humanitarian group *Smiles for Central America*. This team of dental and medical professionals, and other volunteers, travels to countries in Central America twice a year to provide services. This wonderful non-profit group also provides community service in the cities they are serving in. While in San Pedro Sula, Honduras, I provided oral hygiene care to many beautiful Hondurans, and our group saw a total of 660 people.

Before we arrived, they transformed a local church building into a clinic—AMAZING! All of the pew seats were removed and portable dental equipment was brought in. The number of volunteers varied from city to city. Our group consisted of 21 dentists, 4 dental hygienists, 5 endodontists, 1 orthodontist, 5 oral surgeons, 5 doctors, and 1 physician assistant. Many of the people we saw had never been to a medical or dental professional. Although some were scared, they were all deeply grateful to receive the care given to them! They kept saying, "*Gracias,*" or "*Thank you*" in broken English.

There was a local team in San Pedro Sula that provided support for our equipment, food, translation needs, and other things. Every clinician that needed a translator was provided one. I was touched by my interactions with so many of these beautiful young people, but four of them made a particularly lasting imprint on my heart! Marcella was 15 years old and spoke English very well. She was a hard worker and a very fun soul. We would listen to Salsa music from my phone and dance around in the clinic. It didn't take long before a few were calling me the dancing hygienist! Her parents were part of the local team that helped us and were true angels. Marcella and her brother, Sam, both translated in the clinic and worked with a "go get 'em" mentality. I know that this attitude will carry them far in life.

Andrea was another translator I fell in love with because of her positive infectious personality. Her English skills helped me tremendously!

The fourth inspiring young person I met was Joseph. He had been a recipient of these services four years prior, and now he wanted to give back to those who had helped him in his life. He started his studies to be a dentist. This young man simply wanted to be in a position to help others, just as he had been helped. He was taking advantage of a micro-credit program through our church called the Perpetual Education Fund, where young adults are given financial assistance for college tuition. They pay it back upon completion of their education. I felt such love for these wonderful young Hondurans who came from humble backgrounds, and yet radiate such happiness!

One of my favorite days of the whole trip was Sunday. We went to church in San Pedro Sula and brought each family and child some fun things made with love. It was like an early Christmas for them!

A few of the more memorable gifts and moments, I listed specifically in my personal journal:

- For those over the age of 12 they received a journal.
- For those boys and men over the age of 12 they received a shirt and tie.
- For the women over the age of 18 they got beautiful handmade quilts.
- For those over the age of 12 they got handmade jewelry (youth from the states made all of the jewelry).
- Soccer balls for the youth and play clothes for the young children. They were so excited to put on their Zorro costumes and the little princess outfits. It was awesome to watch them—it was like Christmas morning for these children.
- Family photos were taken for each family, which were printed and framed for them that very day! ☺ These parents were so touched that they shed tears of joy. For some of these families, it was their first picture taken together.
- I was assigned to the 'boutique' room and got to hand out jewelry to the women 18 and older. They were so happy and grateful to receive these gifts. When we were boarding our shuttles to leave, we saw many kids laughing, kicking soccer balls, and wearing Zorro costumes and princess dresses! ☺
- It was awesome to mingle with these families. Even though it was hot and humid during church services, with lots of mosquitoes and no air conditioning, we felt right at home with these beautiful people who shared our faith in Jesus Christ. I truly loved this day!

Later that evening, we attended a special sermon by a local preacher who spoke about Christ and his life of service. The meeting also encouraged families to take advantage of the free services that we offered while we were there that week.

Many wonderful things were shared and witnessed about at this meeting, and it was inspiring for all who attended. A local ecclesiastical leader living in Central America spoke about what we were doing in Honduras on what they called a 'Brigade,' and what our purpose was. He was filled with the Spirit. He told them we had come on our own time and dime. The following is a brief paraphrasing from my journal:

> This great spiritual leader, José Alonso, strongly witnessed that Christ lives! That He is loving and knows us by name! José also said, *"I testify HE knows how to smile! HE is real,"*—he shared great appreciation for the grace of Jesus Christ—that those in our group from *Smiles for Central America* are here to share their time, talents, and love and are here to bring the smile of Jesus. They are here to share the plain manifestation of Jesus because He loves us. José talked about the Savior's love, and how His love purified those in ancient times because of their faith.

He witnessed of the life of Christ, how He prayed without ceasing. Again, HE SMILED UPON those He taught. José Alonso then invited the youth to kneel down that night and ask the Lord, "Do you love me?" He said, "You need to have confirmation from the Spirit. I testify that those who are with this group will bring you the smile of Jesus!" 😊 (I was so humbled to hear this, and it changed the spirit and tone of our group for the rest of the trip. We were on the Lord's errand to be an extension of his love!) Later that evening, we realized our group was blessed, that our bodies could go beyond our capacity, our eyes could see with our head lights, and we would be blessed beyond our capabilities. *All of these blessings were fulfilled!* José continued on…"God has answers to life's problems! These people who are here to serve will love you and bring the love and smile of Jesus to the people of Honduras!" 😊

It was amazing as the week progressed, we were blessed far beyond our capacity and provided long days of clinical work. The schedule included very long hours and was challenging ergonomically. A few more notes from my journal about the many wonderful opportunities we had to bring the smile of Jesus to others:

Monday, November 24, 2014: Another amazing day! Everyone in our group is invited to go on a different mini humanitarian trip. Today my group went on ours to a newborn clinic in town at a local hospital. I got to snuggle with lots of babies! There were two units: one was an

Bringing the Smile of Jesus to Others

adolescent unit with teen moms, and the other was for moms over 18 years old. We gave everyone newborn kits. They were so appreciative. We told them these kits were made and given to them with love. It was such a joy to hand them out. Every mother was given a stuffed animal for their baby as well. The newborn kits had diapers, onesies, a receiving blanket, booties, handmade hats, and beautiful handmade quilts. The babies were so precious and had so much hair! Right after the women delivered their babies, they were immediately whisked away and carried to a huge recovery room where they were placed on basic bed sheets. Anything else they needed, they had to bring themselves (clothes for the baby, nursing bra, etc.). The ladies were so happy to receive the newborn kits! 😊 We also saw the NICU clinic. It had maybe half the resources we have in the USA. Kathy, a high school teacher, was our translator for the day. She was wonderful and a fantastic translator. This was such a special trip and day!

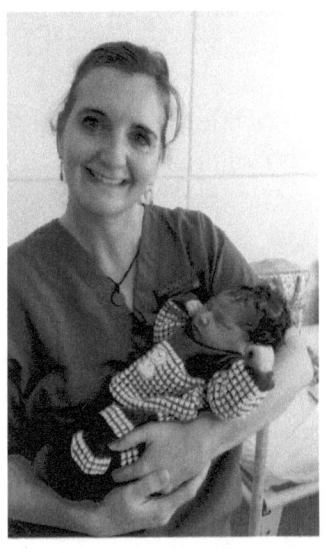

The woman in the photo on the following page is Terra Taylor, a friend and fellow dental hygienist I met on the trip. On her mini humanitarian trip, she visited a children's hospital and saw children who had cancer. Their group brought the children fun toys and gadgets, and they absolutely loved them. In Terra's words, "The opportunity to visit, serve, and touch these beautiful and precious souls was a choice blessing in my life. The recipients expressed heartfelt gratitude that I have only felt while serving on these humanitarian trips. Their gifts to me are so much greater than anything I could ever give or do for them. They are real people who touched my heart with a profound feeling of love, joy, appreciation, and healing that I hope to pass on to the world." More entries from my journal from that day and the following days:

Monday, November 24, 2014: Today at the clinic, we saw a total of 165 young men and women. I saw so many wonderful kids. Some were anxious, some had recently come to know Christ. One had been living on the streets until a few months ago, when he met missionaries and turned his life over to Christ. He is now excited to tell others about Christ and his life. He was so inspiring to me!

With me today were Marcella and Joseph, two fantastic translators. ☺ VERY TIRED. This trip was so awesome—but we had long days, and having to use a headlight for our dental work was physically challenging.

Bringing the Smile of Jesus to Others

Tuesday, November 25, 2014: Today was our busiest day, but it was a great day. We saw a total of 207 kids. My neck and back are super sore and tired—it was a 16-hour day. I know Heavenly Father blessed us beyond our capacity today for sure. Even our equipment was not made to run that many hours without breaking down. I really loved working with all our amazing translators!

Wednesday, November 26, 2014: Last day of clinic. We saw 98 patients—*which makes a total of 660 patients for the week! That is simply a miracle!* 😊 It was absolutely amazing helping others and being an extension of God's love!

When these beautiful Hondurans left the clinic, all of their medical and dental needs had been addressed.

I am grateful for opportunities to serve others and to think outside myself while enduring the 'waits' in life! Think about your life and how you can best be an angel to others during *your waits* and your 'holding patterns' in life! We are all at different places in life, whether you are in a painful wait, or pushing through the everyday mundane in life, there is help from heaven and work to do. We have an abundant life to live!

Army veteran and former Executive Vice President of the University of Utah, Neal Maxwell (1926-2004) said, "Mortality involves teeth to be brushed, beds to be made, cars to be repaired, diapers to be changed, groceries to be bought—such an endless array of mundane matters. In the midst of these, however, is the real business of living—a friendship to be formed, a marriage to be mended, a child to be encouraged, a truth to be driven home, an apology to be made, a Christian attribute to be further developed." (Neal A. Maxwell, Quote Book, 217)

CHAPTER 2

Ministering Angels Seen and Unseen

"For he shall give his angels charge over thee, to keep thee in all thy ways." (Psalm 91:11)

"And, lo, the angel of the Lord came upon them, and the glory of the Lord shone round about them: and they were sore afraid. And the angel of the Lord said unto them, Fear not: for, behold, I bring you good tidings of great joy, which shall be to all people." (Luke 2:9-10)

Part of living with intention in life is being open to being an angel, or an answer to someone's prayer. We often seek God's Spirit to know how to help others through difficult times in their lives. When I was living away from home doing missionary work, I received some devastating news that my mother had terminal ovarian cancer. My mother was amazing through the whole thing and showed a tremendous amount of faith! She wanted me to continue my missionary work. She told me as long as I stayed where I was, doing missionary work, she knew that she would have God's special care.

Fast forward fifteen months later. Up to this point, there had been some really difficult days where we didn't know if my mom was going to make it through the night where many tears were shed and prayers were given. But, I always knew I should stay in Illinois (the area where I was ministering). My mom was insistent that I should not come home. Then, a miracle happened—about nine months after her diagnosis, my mother was going into remission! I felt such relief and continued in my work.

Sometime afterward, I received a phone call from my mom telling me that her cancer was back with a vengeance, and that her doctor thought she had less than a month to live. I could hear my mom crying on the phone. It pained me to the very core. I had tears streaming down my face, but I wouldn't let her hear me cry. I was trying to be strong for her. After calls with my family and mentor friends, I hung up and was physically ill from this distressing development in my mother's health. My roommate at the time and dear friend, Heather Rothey, was with me when I received the phone call from my mom. Heather wanted to comfort me and tried to hug me, but I pulled away. I knew if I started crying, I would not be able to stop. I wanted to go to bed and not talk about anything.

That night as we were getting ready for bed, Heather wanted to have our usual evening prayers. I didn't want to say one, because I knew if I talked, I would start to cry. Heather said the prayer…a few things we both remember…"Heavenly Father, I pray in the name of Jesus Christ that thou wilt bless

Michelle and if possible let me help carry the burden she is carrying. Help her to trust me and know she can tell me all she is feeling. Help her to know she is supposed to go home and be with her mom at this time." She expressed our love to Him and her love for me and asked again to bless her that she could help carry my burden and make it lighter for me. During the prayer, the Spirit was so strong that I started to weep. I sobbed like a baby. I felt so much sadness, pressure, and stress. Heather and I were like sisters—she held me like a baby, and I cried most of the night. I think I shed all the tears that I held in since my mom was diagnosed 14 months earlier. God's miracle came and Heather helped carry my burden and made it lighter. She was an extension of the Lord's love to me! She was my angel friend! *The Lord truly granted her prayer.*

In talking recently with Heather, she said that she has never had that kind of experience since, that is, to be able to truly feel and completely carry the burden of another. It was a very powerful moment and I felt the love of the Lord. This was in January of 1991.

I returned home that week. Sadly, my mother passed away two weeks later.

More Angels Among Us

It was May of 1992, I was living with a dear friend named Katrina who had recently accepted Christ in her life. Katrina was a delightful roommate and we had become fast friends! One day I had been missing my mom terribly, was feeling discouraged with my life, and was dealing with a recent breakup. I went to bed with pensive and heavy thoughts. For the first time in a long time, I slept very sound that night.

Although I didn't see her, I truly felt like I had been comforted by my mother's spirit. I couldn't quite remember, but I awoke feeling much lighter than the previous day. As I went into our living room, Katrina was waiting for me to share what she had experienced during the night. This is her account written in the back of my journal as a second witness (shared with her permission):

> "While fast asleep one night, I awoke startled, with a feeling of spirit filling the apartment. My thoughts were clear and vivid, "There are angels in my room!" Again, later I awoke, *"There are angels definitely in my room!"* I couldn't see them nor did I know who it was. That morning, I told Michelle of my experience and how great and wonderful I felt, how close I felt to the Lord's wonderful mysterious other world. She explained that her mother had visited her that night and I knew it was the truth. She had been there to console and comfort her daughter whom I'm sure she watched over continuously. I bear witness of the truth of Christ's gospel and am grateful for such a marvelous experience that brought me closer to the veil." (Katrina McCloskey Troutman, 1992)

I also remember Katrina telling me that she thought someone left the light on in the hall because she could see light through the base of her door—there was no light on in the hall. Talking with Katrina recently, she said, "This was such a strengthening experience as a new member in Christ. I can never deny that angels are real and they are among us."

Ministering Angels Seen and Unseen

In the spring of 1998, I took a wonderful trip to the Holy Land with a dear friend, Cathy Larsen. It was incredible to walk where Jesus walked. We had many great experiences traveling all around the Sea of Galilee, Jericho, Bethlehem, the Dead Sea, etc. Our group's visit to the Mount of Olives in Jerusalem was pleasantly surprising as well. There is a beautiful pathway that leads to the Garden of Gethsemane. I walked and looked out over the city Jerusalem. I experienced such a peaceful feeling while walking along this pathway. It wasn't a big impression, but I knew my mother's spirit was with me. It was a sweet tender mercy of the Lord. The interesting thing was, when we were back at the bus, Cathy and I were talking about the day and I told her about my experience. Cathy said that she too had felt her brother's presence who had died two years earlier in a tragic hiking accident. Another lady on the bus overheard us talking about this. Amazed, she told us that she too had felt her deceased mother's presence there. It is a sacred place! This was such a loving reminder, as well as a witness to me that our loved ones are with us more than we know!

Many times in our lives, we will have the opportunity to be angels to others. The Lord has blessed me tremendously with angelic friends, kindred friends—truly lifelong friends. I challenge each of us to call upon ministering angels daily to help us, and to look for opportunities to be angels to others.

> "A man that hath friends must shew himself friendly." (Proverbs 18:24)

CHAPTER 3

Loving Our Neighbors

*"Go out into the world today and love the people you meet.
Let your presence light new light in the hearts of others."*
Mother Teresa

Who is our neighbor? After the 2016 Presidential race, I think we were all feeling exhausted from the countless negative ads, comments, and unacceptable behavior from all sides. The Lord would want us to choose better. I believe if we disagree on political, religious, or other issues, we can agree to disagree—but we don't have to be disagreeable!

Jesus taught this lesson well in the beautiful parable of the Good Samaritan in Luke 10:29-35. A certain lawyer asked Jesus, "Who is my neighbor?" And then the story goes on: a man who travels from Jerusalem to Jericho, gets attacked by thieves. They steal from him, beat him, and leave him half dead. A priest and a Levite (who think differently on issues in life) both pass by him on the other side of the road—purposely avoiding him. Then, a Samaritan comes and "had compassion on him" as the scripture says. He probably scooped him up in his arms, tore part of his own clothing to use as a cloth to stop any bleeding, bound up his wounds, and gently carried him to shelter. He offered to pay for his stay and any other expenses that might accrue. Think of our lives today—there are millions of people in this world. We are all different from one another, look different from one another and have different customs, cultures, and beliefs. Isn't it wonderful? But, I also believe WE ARE MORE ALIKE THAN WE ARE DIFFERENT! God loves and knows ALL His children here on earth. That is a fact!

> "At the end of our lives, we will not be judged by how many diplomas we have received, how much money we have made or how many great things we have done. We will be judged by 'I was hungry and you gave me meat. I was naked and you clothed me. I was homeless and you took me in.' " (Mother Teresa)

For a few months in the summer of 2015, I had been trying to reach my friend Jill, who had experienced a painful divorce and was now struggling with her faith. After a few attempts, I finally got through to her on the phone. Our first conversation in July didn't exactly create what you would call 'warm fuzzies.'

Our conversation went like this: "Hi Jill, it's Michelle." There was a hesitant pause from Jill, "Oh...(awkward pause)...Hi." I could tell by the sound of her voice she wished she hadn't answered the phone, she might have even rolled her eyes. I asked if I could briefly visit her. She said, "You don't need to come, I don't even go to church anymore. You don't really need to come." I said, in the kindest voice I could, "I know I don't need to come, but I'd love to come for just five minutes to say hello." She then replied, "Well, you don't really need to. Besides, I am a school teacher and I am off for the next three weeks on a road trip with a friend, so I won't be around." I felt very directed by the Spirit to say, "Oh, that sounds fun! I'll tell you what, why don't you go on your road trip and when you get back we can take that five minutes of you telling me about your trip." With a defiant voice, she said, "Oh, okay, you can just get a hold of me when I get back." After our conversation, I went to the local store and bought a few hand wipes, licorice, and just a few simple things for her road trip. I left them on her door in a little bag with a simple 'have a fun and safe trip' note.

About a month later (and after several attempts to align our schedules), we finally met up. When I first went to her apartment, she invited me in with some caution. I asked her to tell me about her recent trip. I realized it had been close to five minutes that I had been there. I told Jill that it had been five minutes and asked if I could share a brief message before I left. I had no idea what I was going to say, since I had planned on just hearing about her road trip. She hesitantly agreed to let me share a message. Under the direction of the Almighty, I said, "Jill, ever since we talked in July, I have felt strongly that God knows your name and speaks it often. I know Heavenly Father wants you to come back to church, and I need you to tell me what my role is in helping this happen." Jill immediately softened and shared how she had really struggled with her faith due to certain challenges that had weighed heavily on her heart. She went on to say that she just didn't have faith anymore. She said it was too hard to believe there was hope. I told her I knew why God had me contact her. I shared with her that I was 46 years old, never married or had children, and that there was nothing more in life that I wanted than that. I told her I didn't know why that blessing had not come into my life, but I had two choices—I could choose to despair and be discouraged (I told her I've done that and that is not a happy path), or I could choose to trust God even though I couldn't see ahead. I told her I didn't know why we must struggle with the things that we do, but God knows and He love us. I told her I now knew why God had sent me to visit her. I challenged her to hold onto her faith, dig deep, and not let go!

Jill slowly came back to church and began meeting with our local church leader for some spiritual council. She started changing her social life decisions by associating with others who were uplifting.

About three months after I first met with her, I taught a lesson at church on helping others come to Christ. There was a fantastic quote from the church manual that talked about not giving up on each other and being persistent in helping others come to Christ. Jill raised her hand and said, "Can I make a comment?" Jill then shared with the class how she and I had met, and how I wouldn't give up on her and wouldn't take no for an answer. She was emotional as she talked about the changes she was making with the help from the Spirit and her church leader. Many in the class were touched by her sensitive story.

I share this so that we may realize that we *never* know when God will use us to help someone else. We never know when *He* needs us to bring *His* smile to others! At this time in my life, I had started to wonder if God had forgotten me. I had been feeling very discouraged that God didn't need me, or that He didn't have any purpose for me. I am grateful for the Savior's command to love thy neighbor as thyself!

> "How we treat other people can have a great impact on the degree of blessings and favor of God we are experiencing in our lives. Are you good to people? Are you kind and considerate? Do you speak and act with love in your heart and regard other people as valuable and special? Friend, you can't treat people poorly and expect to be blessed. You can't be rude and inconsiderate and expect to live in victory."[1]

A few days after my dad passed away from cancer in 2007, I was sitting on the couch at home feeling paralyzed by my grief—having now lost both of my parents. My dear friend, Angie Lawrence, knocked at my door. I remember she asked what she could do to serve me. I was in such a state that I couldn't think of anything. I did, however, have a basket full of laundry and couldn't get myself to do it. It was too much, it required too much energy. I was literally unable to function. Angie grabbed that basket and did my laundry and a few other things during that visit. I will forever be grateful for her kindness and her selfless gesture! It was such a great example of extending the Lord's love to others, by being an earthly angel!

Loving Our Neighbors

I learned a long time ago that no matter how hard life gets, we *always* need the Lord and our fellowship with those who share our belief in Him. C.S. Lewis constantly refers to Satan as the enemy. One thing I know for sure is that the enemy wants nothing more than to hold us back from reaching out to others and being where God wants us to be. We can't afford to not have His Spirit with us! We never know when the Lord needs us to bring the smile of Jesus to others.

One observation I have is that so many of us are extremely busy. I know because I live a busy life too. But it amazes me that some will find time to watch *The Bachelor* on TV, weekly sporting events (or in my case, *Dancing with the Stars*) and yet, they can't find time to visit and minister to others.

While associating with other single Christians, I had two friends that came to see me during a difficult time. Dave and Drew were dedicated friends. Drew has mild intellectual disabilities and really wanted to serve others. Dave and Drew would come to see me from time to time and were especially wonderful during a period when I was very sick with a virus. During that time, they came over and prayed with me, and also gave me a beautiful blessing. Drew wasn't quite sure what to say. Dave helped Drew know what to say word for word. It was so sweet to see this humble soul wanting to be God's instrument.

CHAPTER 4

Trust the Lord and Call Upon Angels

"The love of God is greater far. Than tongue or pen can ever tell. It goes beyond the highest star. And reaches to the lowest hell. The guilty pair, bowed down with care. God gave His Son to win. His erring child He reconciled. And pardoned from his sin…Could we with ink the ocean fill? Was the whole Earth of parchment made? And every single stick a quill and every man a scribe by trade? To write the love of God above would drain the ocean dry, nor could the whole upon the scroll—be spread from sky to sky."
Frederick M. Lehman[2]

I testify that God lives, that He knows each of us by name. I love this beautiful saying above of how *He* feels about us! I want to share one of my favorite scriptures in the *Old Testament*. Shadrach, Meshach, and Abednego will not deny the God of Israel and are about to face possible death and be cast into the furnace of fire:

Trust the Lord and Call Upon Angels

If it be so, our God whom we serve is able to deliver us from the burning fiery furnace, and he will deliver us out of thine hand, O king.

...that we will not serve thy gods, nor worship the golden image which thou hast set up.

Then was Nebuchadnezzar full of fury...commanded that they should heat the furnace one seven times more than it was wont to be heated.

And he commanded the most mighty men that were in his army to bind Shadrach, Meshach, and Abednego, and to cast them into the burning fiery furnace.

Then these men were bound in their coats, their hosen, and their hats, and their other garments, and were cast into the midst of the burning fiery furnace.

Therefore because the king's commandment was urgent, and the furnace exceeding hot, the flames of the fire slew those men that took up Shadrach, Meshach, and Abednego.

And these three men, Shadrach, Meshach, and Abednego, fell down bound into the midst of the burning fiery furnace.

Then Nebuchadnezzar the king was astonished... and spake, and said unto his counsellors, Did not we cast three men bound into the midst of the fire? They answered and said unto the king, True, O king.

He answered and said, Lo, I see four men loose, walking in the midst of the fire, and they have no hurt; and the form of the fourth is like the Son of God.

Then Nebuchadnezzar came...and spake, and said, Shadrach, Meshach, and Abednego, ye servants of the most high God, come forth, and come hither. Then Shadrach, Meshach, and Abednego, came forth of the midst of the fire.

And the princes, governors, and captains, and the king's counsellors, being gathered together, saw these men, upon whose bodies the fire had no power, nor was an hair of their head singed, neither were their coats changed, nor the smell of fire had passed on them. (Daniel 3:16-27)

Growing up close to the Oregon Coast, I was privileged several times to enjoy a wonderful campfire at the beach with friends. Usually, after being around a campfire, the smell of fire is in your hair, skin, and clothes. The smell doesn't go away until after you shower. But here, Shadrach, Meshach, and Abednego had not even a hair on their head singed and even the smell of fire had passed by them. I know God the Father and His Son, Jesus Christ, *will also stand with us* through *any* furnace that is placed before us! The Enemy has a big lie out there that we are buying into—that God has abandoned us, forgotten us, or we are alone here trying to make it through this mortality. That is absolutely not true! God has not, CANNOT, and WILL NOT abandon us! They—God the Father and Jesus Christ—love us, know us by name and speak our names often. That is God's truth! I want to share this truth with you.

To quote Neal Maxwell again, "The thermostat on the furnace of affliction will not have been set too high for us—though clearly we may think so at the time. Our God is a refining God who has been *tempering soul-steel for a very long time.* He knows when the right edge has been put upon our excellence and also when there is more in us than we have yet given. One day we will praise God for taking us near to our limits—as He did His Only Begotten in Gethsemane and Calvary."

"We will also see that our lives have been fully and fairly measured. In retrospect, we will even see that our most trying years here will often have been our best years, *producing large tree rings on our soul,* Gethsemanes of growth!"[3]

I want to share with you two of the many times God the Father and Jesus Christ have stood with me through a difficult trial—a furnace of affliction. First, I refer back to the news of my mom's cancer diagnosis while living away from home. It was the week before Christmas. For a few weeks, my heart had been heavy with thoughts about home, and I didn't know why. On this particular day, we had been blessed with about a foot and half of snow in Illinois. As my roommate and I were walking in the door of our apartment, we heard the phone ringing. I immediately felt sick to my stomach and knew that it was for me. I took the phone and said hello. I heard my sister Mattye state gravely, "You may want to sit down Michelle." "Is it Mom?" I asked. She answered, "How did you know?" "I don't know, I just know something is wrong!" I said. She proceeded to tell me that my mother had ovarian cancer that had spread to her lungs and the prognosis was not good. They were saying she had about 4-6 months to live. She was scheduled for a radical hysterectomy and chemotherapy treatments in the upcoming weeks. My sister gave me a few more details, and we agreed to talk again in a few days on Christmas.

When I hung up the phone, Lori, my roommate and friend, came over and wrapped her arms around me. Emotionally, I felt as if I'd been hit with a golf club! I went into the bathroom and was sick. I felt so many emotions overwhelming me. I told Lori that I needed to be alone and went into the bedroom. I fell on the bed and cried and cried. I thought my heart would literally break. After what felt like hours later, she came into the room, put her arms around me and said, "Michelle, we are going to make it through this together with the Savior's help." She hugged me one more time, then left the room.

I slipped off the bed straight to my knees and prayed like I never had before. I poured my soul out to Heavenly Father, pleading for Him to help me! After a time, I remember looking up, and on the wall above my bed was a framed art drawing of Jesus in the Garden of Gethsemane. Eventually, I felt as if His loving arms were wrapped around me, letting me know that no matter what happened, I would be okay because of His grace and redeeming power. He truly was bearing my grief and carrying my sorrows (Isaiah 53:4). I wasn't sure how, but I knew with my Savior and Heavenly Father's help, I would somehow make it through this painful time.

Fast forward to 2010: I had a very unhealthy, toxic situation at work that I needed to remove myself from. After much prayer and talking with my ecclesiastical leader, I knew I needed to leave my job. This was not logical at all, as I didn't have another job lined up. Nonetheless, this was the clear answer from the Lord. The morning I was to give my notice, I was praying and started to cry. I felt a bit like the Red Sea was ahead of me. I could barely focus on anything, but I thought that I should read one scripture for my study that morning. I was reading a little about the life of Jesus, and great peace came to my mind. It was a beautiful witness from God that I would be okay. That day I went to work and gave my two-week notice. During this time, I was blessed to find temporary work as a dental hygienist and as a house cleaner and sitter. I did whatever I could to make ends meet until I found a job. Four months later, I began to become discouraged and started to feel panicked. I went to one of my best friend's houses and she and her husband prayed with me. My friend said to me, "Michelle, I feel impressed to tell you, God is in charge and He will bring peace to your life. It will all be okay!" 😊 I started to get a little weepy. Was God in the details of my life?—ABSOLUTELY! Is He in the details of my life today? The answer is YES! Is He in the details of your life? YES!

"The mercy, O Lord, is in the heavens;
and thy faithfulness reacheth unto the clouds.
How excellent is thy loving kindness, O God!"
(Psalms 36:5, 7)

"The Lord is gracious, and full of compassion;
Slow to anger, and of great mercy.
The Lord is good to all:
and His tender mercies are over all His works."
(Psalms 145:8-9)

I also want to attest that we can call upon ministering angels to help us. Although I have never seen them, I know that both of my parents who have passed on have helped me from time to time.

Hardship will come to all of us in life. I promise that if you dig deep, stay the course, keep praying, keep participating in worship, keep searching the word of God, DON'T give up your faith, and hold on, God will NOT abandon you! He loves us too much and is there through every hardship.

Dale Carnegie said it well when he said, "Most of the important things in the world have been accomplished by people who have kept on trying when there seemed to be no hope at all."[4] We must reach out to others. God will stand with you through *any* furnace of affliction! *We must trust in the Lord* through adversity.

> "And I will walk among you, and will be your God, and ye shall be my people. I am the Lord your God…" (Leviticus 26:12-13)

I know this is true, for God is a perfect God and a God of truth and *He cannot lie!* "I will not leave you comfortless: I will come to you." (John 14:18).

CHAPTER 5

Appreciate Liberty!

*Our freedom was won long ago by men young and men gray.
Their courage was strong, they fought for their faith,
And they were quick with no delay!
Next time you vote or kneel to God to offer your soul to pray,
Remember those heroes of long ago,
That paved freedom's way.*

    I wrote these words several years ago while I was visiting Massachusetts. I was touched as I stepped back in time and took the journey from Lexington to Concord. I learned there that three generations of families fought on the same day. Sons, fathers, and grandfathers all fought in the war that paved freedom's way!

    It has been my privilege to travel to many historical sites in the United States. I have visited the Statue of Liberty, Independence Hall, Washington D.C., Plymouth Rock, Pearl Harbor, and Gettysburg. One cannot travel to these places without feeling a deep appreciation for our country and the men and women who have sacrificed their lives for our freedom. Whenever I visit places like these, I try to buy a book that tells the history of the site, even if it's just an educational children's book with photographs or illustrations. I always feel a deep sense of gratitude and love for my country when I read these inspiring books of famous places in my collection.

Being an American is a great blessing, especially as a woman. In many countries, women have no voice at all, no opportunities. In 2002 on the streets of Ho Chi Minh City, Vietnam, a three-year-old girl tried to sell me a package of gum and some cigarettes. What is the future for that girl? I lost sleep over that little girl! Here in America, women can own land, vote, and follow their dreams. They can also receive an education. I know there are many places in the world that this is true, but my point is, it is a blessing!

Recently, I read a book called *My Forbidden Face*, a memoir of a young woman living under Taliban rule in Afghanistan. The author, who calls herself only "Latifa," writes about how women were mostly confined to their homes, and when they did go outside, they were required by law to wear a burka, (a veil that covers the face and hair). According to Latifa, Afghani women suffered many atrocities. For example, Latifa writes of a teenage girl who had her fingers chopped off because she wore fingernail polish. Latifa watched her mother, a physician, assist women in childbirth as well as tend to their other medical needs, all done in secret in their homes. Men were not allowed to deliver babies, yet women were prevented by law from openly practicing medicine. Consequently, women would go through labor and childbirth without medical assistance or

Appreciate Liberty!

help, and many women and infants died as a result. Latifa's mother would have been imprisoned and possibly tortured or executed if she were caught practicing medicine, but out of her own humanity, she did it anyway.

When the Taliban took over the Afghani government, many opportunities for females—including education—became illegal. For over a year, Latifa felt powerless. Finally, with great determination, she decided to follow her mother's incredible courage and started a small school in her home. Although this was illegal, Latifa couldn't stand the thought of the young girls in her apartment complex not learning how to read. This continued for several years, during which time Latifa miraculously gained access to the books her students needed.

To take a stand for something good is one thing, but doing so when you could be tortured or executed for it is another thing entirely. I am grateful for our local libraries where I am free to check out a book—any book I want—and read it. Although this seems like a simple thing, think how often we take even our local libraries for granted. In Afghanistan, and in other countries, books were often burned. This is still the case in some countries.

Another great way we can *be angels while we wait* in life is to live in appreciation of these many freedoms we have here in America—freedom of religion, freedom of speech, freedom to receive an education, to vote, and countless others.

Former U.S. Secretary of Agriculture, and spiritual leader, Ezra Benson stated in an address given in 1986 on the Constitution, "Look back in retrospect on almost six thousand years of human history. Freedom's moments have been infrequent and exceptional. We must appreciate that we live in one of history's most exceptional moments—in a nation and a time of unprecedented freedom. Freedom as we know it has been experienced by perhaps less than one percent of the human family!"[5] Just an interesting side note, three years after this talk was given, the Berlin Wall came down overnight!

I sit on the State of Utah's Refugee Health Advisory Board. Some of these refugees have been victims of torture and violence. Some of the refugee mothers want to help their children learn to read and write in America, but they are not literate themselves because they did not have the right to be educated. I realize that as a woman in America, I am extremely privileged. I am grateful for my education and again, for the fact that I have a library card in my purse that I can use anytime I want to check out any book I would like.

My job gives me the privilege to provide dental screenings and oral health education to refugees. While meeting with a group of refugees in an "English as a Second Language (ESL)" class, we gave each participant a toothbrush, floss, and toothpaste. One lady said she would be happy to share this toothbrush with her family. I kindly instructed her they should each have their own. I then learned from her that while they spent several years in a refugee camp, they shared a single toothbrush and washcloth with the whole family. I silently thanked Heavenly Father for the many blessings I enjoy every day and take for granted.

LET US EXPAND OUR HEARTS WITH
GRATITUDE FOR ALL THAT WE HAVE!

Appreciate Liberty!

In April of 2016, I spoke at the National Oral Health conference in Cincinnati, Ohio. I fell in love with the city as I walked along the Ohio River and saw the lush green grass and trees that line it. While there, I visited the National Underground Railroad Freedom Center. I was truly touched by this place and it made a deep imprint on my heart! It's main purpose and tribute (stated in the museum) is "to abolish human enslavement and secure freedom for all people." I was inspired by tributes to the lives of so many courageous people from the past, like: Harriet Tubman, Frederick Douglass, Harriet Beecher Stowe and countless others who were instrumental in freeing slaves during the 1800s.

There were two sisters I had not previously heard of, Sarah and Angelina Grimke. They were Caucasian women from the South who were proactive abolitionists and showed great courage during the vile, horrible time of slavery. Both were witnesses as children to the cruelty of slavery. They watched slaves labor past the point of exhaustion in corn and cotton fields. They both secretly taught slaves how to read, wrote letters and pamphlets against slavery, sat with slaves in church services, and were voices for the women's suffrage movement later in their lives. I was grateful for these women who were a voice for those who did not have a voice. For more information on these two sisters, visit www.nps.gov.12.

Other things that were sobering to learn (information taken from the Underground Railroad Freedom Center):

- There are more slaves today, worldwide, than were seized from Africa in four centuries of the trans-Atlantic slave trade. Human trafficking and illegal drug trafficking have a global reach. Millions of dollars are made each year from these horrors that destroy lives.

- The chocolate industry is worth an estimated $110 billion a year, and yet, it's key commodity is grown by some of the poorest children in the world who have been taken into slave labor.
- Unfortunately, enslavement and human trafficking are not things of the past. Human trafficking is the fastest-growing international crime.
- Millions of girls around the world face barriers to education.
- There are countries where there is literally no freedom at all—such as North Korea. Males and females are equally oppressed. There is no freedom of speech, religion, education, or choice of any kind, things most of us in the U.S. have been blessed with for years.
- There are more than 43 million displaced refugees throughout the world.
- At the Underground Railroad Freedom Center, they advertised a new documentary that puts a spotlight on child trafficking called *The Abolitionists*, sharing ideas on how you can help support those who are fighting trafficking.
- Harriet Tubman made 13 trips to free over 70 slaves. She had some serious courage, especially when there was a bounty on her head.

Appreciate Liberty!

How grateful I am to live in America where I can learn about Jesus and how His life has brought me true freedom. I recently read a book called *Escape from Camp 14: One Man's Remarkable Odyssey from North Korea to Freedom*. This book is about a 23-year-old man who was born in a political camp and basically lived with zero freedom. One of the things that kept him alive was the fact that he knew how to capture rats and eat them. He was beaten or disciplined almost daily. Three generations of his family had been in these camps and he never knew why. I can't even imagine what that must have been like.

Living in this choice land of America comes with great privilege, but it also comes with great responsibilities. I'd like to suggest four things we can do to show appreciation for our liberties, and for the blood that continues to be spilt for us every day so that our freedom might be preserved.

One—Pray for the Leaders of Our Nation and ALL Nations

In addition to personal prayers, we can put our nation's leader's names on church prayer rolls and include them in our fasting and prayers, that they may have and use discernment from God. Many of God's children are being brought to America either as immigrants or refugees. We have a great opportunity to love and serve them. Many have come from very difficult circumstances! The following prayer was given during the 2014 National Day of Prayer by Anne Graham Lotz (daughter of Billie Graham):

> "Lord of the Universe. Lord of this planet. Lord of the nations. Lord of our hearts. On this National Day of

Prayer, we look to YOU…In darkness, You are our Light. In the storm, You are our Anchor. In our weakness, You are our Strength. In our grief, You are our Comfort. In our despair, You are our Hope. In our confusion, You are our Wisdom. In time of terrorism, You are our Shield. In time of War, You are our Peace. In times of uncertainty. You are the Rock on which we stand. We make our prayer to You using the words of the prophet Daniel: O Lord, You are the great and awesome God, who keeps His covenant of love with those who love Him and keep His commandments. You are merciful and forgiving… We have turned away from Your commands and principles. We have turned away from You. Yet, You have promised in Chronicles 7, that if we—a people identified with YOU—would humble ourselves, pray, seek Your face and turn from our wicked ways, then You would hear our prayer, forgive our sins and heal our land…In response to our heartfelt repentance, God of Abraham, Isaac and Jacob, Father of Jesus Christ, in keeping with all Your righteous acts and according to Your promise, turn away Your anger and Your wrath from the United States of America. Hear the prayers and petitions offered… Give ear, our God, and hear; open Your eyes and see. We do not make request of you because we are righteous, but because of Your mercy…For your glory of Your Name hear our prayer, forgive our sins, and heal our land. We ask this in the name of Your Son Jesus Christ who offers us salvation from Your judgment, forgiveness for our sin, and reconciliation with You through His own blood shed on the Cross. Amen."[6]

Appreciate Liberty!

Two—Pray for Our Serving Military and Our Veterans

Let us remember in our daily prayers the men and women who currently serve in the military and those who once served. Pray for them, their families, and reach out to those families who have someone away from home. This can be a very stressful time for them. Their sacrifices are for us and our freedoms!

"All-powerful and ever-living God,
When Abraham left his native land,
and departed from his people,
You kept him safe through all his journeys.
Protect these soldiers, be their constant companion
and their strength in battle,
Their refuge in every adversity.
Guide them, O Lord, that they may
return home in safety.
We ask this through Christ our Lord. Amen."
(United States Conference of Catholic Bishops)[7]

Three—Pray for Those Living in Oppression

Pray for all of those who are living in oppressed lands that have restricted freedom. Pray that hearts will be softened and miracles will bring them to the knowledge of God's love. We have witnessed this miracle over and over again in many countries. We can learn about refugees, see if there are any living in our local areas, and whether there is something we can do to help them. For instance, you can volunteer to help them learn English, or ask a resettlement agency how you can help (www.rescue.org). This photo shows Kaylee, one of my interns, and me teaching refugees about oral hygiene at a Humanitarian Center in Salt Lake City, Utah. "For I was an hungered, and ye gave me meat; I was thirsty, and ye gave me drink; I was a stranger, and ye took me in; Naked, and ye clothed me. I was in prison, and ye came unto me." (Matthew 25:35-36)

Four—We Must Remain Purposeful

Jesus taught us how to live our lives with purpose regardless of how busy our lives are. We read in Mark:

And, behold, there cometh one of the rulers of the synagogue, Jairus by name; and when he saw him, he fell at his feet,

And besought him greatly, saying, My little daughter lieth at the point of death: *I pray thee,* come and lay thy hands on her, that she may be healed; and she shall live.

And *Jesus* went with him; and much people followed him, and thronged him.

And a certain woman, which had an issue of blood twelve years,

And had suffered many things of many physicians, and had spent all that she had, and was nothing bettered, but rather grew worse,

When she had heard of Jesus, came in the press behind, and touched his garment.

For she said, If I may touch but his clothes, I shall be whole.

And straightway the fountain of her blood was dried up; and she felt in *her* body that she was healed of that plague.

And Jesus, immediately knowing in himself that virtue had gone out of him, turned him about in the press, and said, Who touched my clothes?

And his disciples said unto him, Thou seest the multitude thronging thee, and sayest thou, Who touched me? *(I can see them saying Master, look around, there are a lot of people here, many are touching you.)*

And he looked round about to see her that had done this thing.

But the woman fearing and trembling, knowing what was done in her, came and fell down before him, and told him all the truth.

And he said unto her, Daughter, thy faith hath made thee whole; go in peace, and be whole of thy plague. (Mark 5:22-34)

Here we see Jesus was very busy, being whisked away to heal Jairus's daughter, with many people following him, as the scripture says, *thronging* him. He was doing very important work and healing many along the way. Amidst this busy schedule, a faithful woman came along that had struggled with this illness and heavy burden for 12 years. She had such faith in the Savior that she could be healed just by touching his garment. I am sure this was something He was quite used to by now, and since He was dealing with a life and death situation, it would be understandable if he continued swiftly onto Jairus's home. Yet, He did NOT! The entire incident where he stopped to acknowledge this woman's faith probably took about five minutes. Despite His busy schedule, He persisted in purposefulness by acknowledging her faith and putting her mind at ease so she could go in peace. I appreciate the scripture in Proverbs that speaks about staying focused on the Lord's path. "Let thine eyes look right on, and let thine eyelids look straight before thee. Ponder the path of thy feet, and let all thy ways be established. Turn not to the right hand nor to the left: remove thy foot from evil." (Proverbs 4:24-26)

Think of our crazy schedules. Between family, kids, trying to get in personal daily devotions of the good word, work, school, volunteering, church assignments, worship services, everyday errands, trying to get in exercise, etc., do we take time to be purposeful? Do we take a moment to ask the clerk at the store or bank how their day is going? Do we respond to inspiration to reach out to a friend or family member? Again, let us never forget that living in a free nation comes with great privilege and responsibility. Let us remain purposeful as we live in this land of privilege and liberty. Seek to be where God needs you to be, devote your time to good things, bless who you can, and where we can…even amid crazy schedules!

To close the thought of appreciating our liberties, I want to give a list of things we can do while *waiting between now*

Appreciate Liberty!

and when in life. I've spoken of four ways to show more appreciation of our freedoms. Here are a few things we can do to be proactive in sustaining our own liberty and helping others embrace it:

- Be a registered and educated voter and then get out and VOTE!
- Show gratitude to our troops and show support to their families back home.
- Read about our forefathers and learn about American History.
- See www.ourrescue.org to learn how you can help support those who rescue children from sex trafficking.

CHAPTER 6

Testify to Others

"For I know that my redeemer liveth."
(Job 19:26)

In December of 2002 I was preparing for a humanitarian trip to Saigon, Vietnam. It was the day before Christmas, and I was to fly out the next day. I was feeling anxious about the trip and the long flight over an ocean. I asked for a blessing in the form of a prayer. I remember that the prayer included a blessing for a safe trip. Also, a request that the truth of Christ's gospel would be brought to the people of Vietnam, through humanitarian efforts. As the prayer continued, I was told that I would serve pure and noble spirits who were not here on earth to be tested, but to teach love *(Wow!)*. Needless to say, I was comforted as I traveled to the beautiful country of Vietnam.

While in Vietnam, our group had amazing experiences working in orphanages and helping to build a kindergarten in a village located in a city called Hue. Hue is in the central area of Vietnam and is where the epicenter of the war was. I remember the day before we left Vietnam, I thought about the blessing I received at the beginning of this journey, and although I did meet amazing humble people, I was afraid that I may have missed the lesson on love. On our way to the airport, we stopped by a handicapped orphanage in Saigon. There were infants and children living in a way that I hope to never see again. What we saw was horrific! We were taken rather quickly through the orphanage. There was a room where infants were kept. They were alone, and the smell of urine was palatable. Most of the babies were in boxed crates that were saturated with urine. The Buddhist monk (a woman with a shaved head) wanted to keep us moving in the orphanage, as if she knew how horrified we were.

I found it interesting that there was a Buddhist temple next to the orphanage that had fine gold and a lot of money tied into it. Obviously not a cent went to the orphanage.

While everyone left the room with the Buddhist monk, I stayed behind and noticed a tiny infant boy who was maybe five months old. He had an underdeveloped hand and was staring at the wall. There were open sores on his bottom and an open lesion on his inner thighs. We were told not to touch any of the children who had open wounds so we wouldn't pick up any infections. I found a blanket and picked up this *pure and noble spirit*. He was staring off into space, and I could tell was suffering from attachment loss—he had seldom been held and rarely, if at all, changed and cleaned. I snuggled him in my arms and softly started to sing in his ear some Christian hymns. As I was singing, this tiny child slowly moved his head toward me and gazed into my eyes. We had spirit to spirit communication. The Lord wanted me to know through this little child that I was a child of God—*this infant was teaching me who I really was!* It was a very powerful and sacred moment.

A few minutes later, someone from our American group said, "There she is." I looked up and the flash of a camera went off. Someone had taken my picture with this baby. As I looked down on him, he had gone back to staring at nothing. I knew our communication was over. The beautiful blessing had been fulfilled—I had been among pure and noble spirits. This child, I knew, was not here on earth to be tested, but was here to teach love. "The Spirit itself beareth witness with our spirit, that we are children of God." (Romans 8:16)

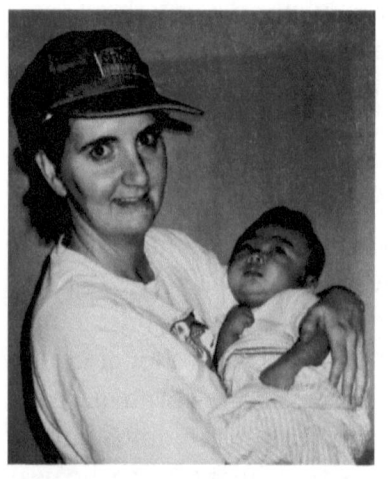

"...and all of you are children of the most High." (Psalms 82:6)

A few Christmases ago, I was in a very dark, lonely place of despair which can happen if I don't stand guard against negative thoughts at the door of my mind. I have a hard time opening myself to others when I am struggling. I was blessed that day to receive a phone call from one of my ministering angel friends, Cara, who called to tell me she was thinking of me and how much she knew that the Lord knew me. I don't remember all that she said, but I do remember the Spirit and love of the Lord that I felt that night—light permeated my soul! Thank goodness for ministering angel friends.

> "God is at work in each of us, whether we know it or not, whether we want it or not." (Max Lucado)[8]

In his family memoir *Faith of My Fathers,* John McCain shares his personal hardship and tragedy of being a prisoner of war in Vietnam. He shares moments of being captured, breaking both of his arms and a leg, suffering continuous physical torture and spending much of his time in solitary confinement enduring neglect during his five and a half years of captivity from 1967 to 1973. He discloses one of his lowest times, being detained in a very small box for solitary confinement. In his own words, he shares, "Once I was thrown into another cell after a long and difficult interrogation. I discovered scratched into one of the cell's walls the creed, *I believe in God, the Father Almighty.* There, standing witness of God's presence in a remote, concealed place, recalled to my faith by a stronger, better man, I felt God's love and care more vividly that I would have felt it had I been safe among a pious congregation in the most magnificent cathedral."

While watching a news broadcast on television one night, I heard John McCain talk about this gruesome, yet bitter sweet account. He said those few scratched words on the wall restored his faith and will to survive.

People like my sweet friend Cara and the man in captivity who wrote those powerful words inside a dark, boxed prison that helped John McCain feel hope, may never know how much their witnessing helps and impacts others. I believe this is true for all of us. We never know the depth of the power that lies in sharing what we know to be true and the potential of being exactly where God needs us! I know God lives, I know Jesus Christ is the Savior of the world, and I know that His grace and love are real. There have been many times where I have struggled or felt low, but I am spiritually invigorated when I bear witness of God and His love.

A closing challenge for this chapter is to share your witness of God and His goodness today! Share it with your family, your spouse, or your roommate. Write it in your journal, share it with a friend at church. Keep your witness simple and based on God and His Son, Jesus Christ. *He lives, all glory to His name.* He lives! He is ever watchful. He knows us by name. Take time to share this knowledge often and you will be strengthened, and will be able to edify others as well.

CHAPTER 7

Trials Can Be Mercies in Disguise

"Be still, and know that I am God."
(Psalms 46:10)

I frequently listen to the Christian radio station KLOVE. There is a song that I love by the talented singer, Laura Story, called "Blessings." This song asks, "What if trials in this life are your mercies in disguise?" The Apostle Paul said he gloried in tribulation, I don't know if I would ever say that! However, I must admit when looking back on the death of my parents and a few other difficult dark times in my life, the trials were, in fact, tender mercies in disguise, even though they were agonizing, emotional times.

In the Fall of 2012, I woke up with a terrible backache on my left side. It hurt all day and I had a little 2-inch rash on my hip. I thought I had injured myself at the gym, but I was so busy with work that I didn't take the time to get myself checked out. The next night, I had to ask a neighbor-friend to take me to the

Emergency Room because I was in such excruciating pain that I thought I was passing a kidney stone or something. After several hours in the ER, I was told I had shingles. What? Shingles? Are you sure? "Isn't that what 80-year-olds get?" I asked. She confirmed that I had shingles and had the classic rash. She sent me home with a prescription and told me to rest.

I had two engagements at work the next week where I was the keynote speaker. I wasn't sure how I could avoid going. So, I filled and used the prescription, but continued with my busy work schedule. All this did was prolong my illness, probably not the smartest choice I had ever made. I had back aches, burning fire on my side, insanely intense headaches, and fatigue. Basically, I had never been so physically miserable in my life. The thought of a semi-truck running me over almost sounded inviting. With all that said, I must admit that it was through this 7-week illness that I was strengthened with heavenly help and experienced some tender mercies.

While dealing with my shingles, my friend picked up a book that I had requested at the library for me. It was the book on CD: *Escape from Camp 14: One Man's Remarkable Odyssey from North Korea to Freedom*. I listened to it all day. Again, this was a true story based on a young man who was raised in a political camp in North Korea with absolutely *no freedom*. He ended up miraculously defecting to China, and eventually making it to South Korea. The atrocities that he, and all those in his camp, endured every day made me disgusted and sad.

At the time, I was studying the teachings of Christ in the scriptures as well and had a great epiphany. Basically, Christ's unconditional love for the people of Jerusalem still exists today for the people of North Korea. I knew He knew all of them by name and He was completely aware of them, of all their pain and suffering. *His redemption covers it all!* And, if He knew their pain and suffering, that could only mean that *He knew mine,* and loved me and wanted to comfort me in my own time of suffering. I know it sounds very simple, but it was so powerful! God knows all of our joys and all of our sufferings. He is completely aware of us.

One of my favorite stories in the Bible is the Lord's deliverance of the children of Israel from the Egyptians. Through the prophet Moses, the Lord shows His power by bringing terrible plagues upon the Egyptians, from painful boils to infestations of frogs, flies, and locusts, to dreadful storms, water turning into blood, and ultimately the death of all Egypt's firstborn children, including Pharaoh's son. Finally, Pharaoh tells the Israelites to depart, which they do, rejoicing. Shortly after leaving Egypt, the Israelites arrive at the shore of the Red Sea. When they see Pharaoh's soldiers coming, the Israelites murmur, already forgetting the miraculous power of their Deliverer. "For it had been better for us to serve the Egyptians, than that we should die in the wilderness" (Exodus 14:12). The Lord just performed miracles to free His children from bondage. How could they forget so easily?

This story relates to us today, because like you, I have faced my own Red Sea. Through times such as these, I've learned that the Lord always knows what is best for us. And somehow, some way, He always parts the Red Sea. But, sometimes when I jump in and start to walk on the dry ground, I look up and see the walls of water. I yank on my backpack to see if my scuba gear is still in there "just in case." Just in case He lets the walls of water fall on me, or in case He leaves me on my own, I guess. And when I have these unrealistic fears, I feel the Lord is asking, "Michelle, don't you remember the other miracles—the frogs, the flies, and the locust?" And I imagine Him saying, "Michelle, put that scuba gear down! Step away and move forward with faith!" We have been taught to be prepared in all things, but when the Lord says to trust Him, trust Him. He is bound to His promise when we do.

GOD IS AWARE OF US AND IS IN THE DETAILS OF OUR LIVES!

While working as a Cancer Information Specialist (Health Educator about Cancer) at the Huntsman Cancer Institute, I had the opportunity to talk with individuals and families about their cancer diagnosis as I helped provide resources for them while they went through their journey with cancer. These families were facing the unknown. Having lost both my parents to cancer, I know that cancer affects the entire family.

I was especially blessed when I became acquainted with Sarah. She was a beautiful mother of six children who lived in Wyoming. She was larger than life and had an infectious smile that brightened everyone's day. She had been diagnosed with multiple myeloma and had received two bone marrow transplants back to back. This is extremely difficult for patients to go through. Sarah found a wonderful place to stay while receiving treatment in Salt Lake City until the doctors cleared her to go home. Her parents also lived out of town and came to stay with her to support her during this difficult time. She received treatment during the holidays, and was away from her sweet family through Christmas. We laughed together, cried together, talked about the deepest things of the soul, and prayed together.

Because Sarah's immune system was so weak and her kids struggled with colds, she was not able to see them that Christmas. I know it was hard for her not to be with her kids on Christmas morning or to be able to make breakfast for them. Sarah missed preparing daily lunches for school, doing their laundry, and all the things she had enjoyed before. What touched me (and her), was how their local church group did so much for her! Someone came over several times a week to do laundry, people brought meals daily, folks took the kids out for ice cream, and members of their church helped every single day with the care of her kids. She found such comfort knowing that there were so many people helping her family while she was gone. What impressed me the most was while she was fighting for her life, Sarah was full of gratitude for Jesus Christ, for those helping her family, her husband, her doctors, her parents, and even me. She exuded appreciation throughout her affliction. She was a wonderful example of faith and hope. Sarah lost her battle with cancer in May 2011. Her funeral was a tribute to a life devoted to following the path of the Savior!

> "Surely he hath born our griefs and carried our sorrows…and with His stripes, we are healed!"
> (Isaiah 53:4, 5)

More Tender Mercies

In the Spring of 2010, I traveled to the beautiful city of Cuzco, Peru for a three-day conference with a non-profit organization called *Reach Out and Learn*. Our purpose was to provide continuing education for medical and dental professionals on various topics. I researched and prepared a presentation on Oral Cancer and the Human papillomavirus (HPV). The rest of the volunteers and I stayed in Cuzco the day we presented and helped out with the conference. On the days we didn't speak, we were taken to a remote village about an hour away from Cuzco at a very high elevation. The people there lived off the land and spoke their tribal language.

I was scheduled to speak the second day of the conference. Consequently, the first day of the trip I was able to join those going up to this remote village. We planned to paint their little school, pass out soccer balls, and have lots of fun giving

Trials Can Be Mercies in Disguise

trinkets and games to the children. We traveled about eight miles up a windy, narrow, and treacherous road. Some of us were struggling with headaches because of the altitude. We were told the road was traveled by a car about once a week, and we were on a bus carrying all of us and our equipment. Looking over the edge around each switchback made me a bit queasy and nervous. I have to admit, I was saying a few silent prayers along the way. The mountain terrain that surrounded us was majestic with several hues of lush greens. It was absolutely stunning! The sunshine was glowing and we were blessed with deep blue skies. I discovered later what a blessing that sunshine truly was for us.

When we were one mile from the village there was a problem with our bus and it completely broke down. We streamed out of the bus, basked in the beauty that surrounded us and took lots of photos. Then we realized the gravity of our situation. The village was still about a mile up the dirt road, and we were approaching 13,000 feet in altitude with lower oxygen levels. Knowing that the dirt road only saw about one car a week, we decided to say a prayer that help would come. We then witnessed a *true miracle*. Within minutes, not *one,* but *two* vehicles were driving up the hill!

During the previous few weeks, the wonderful people of this village had been devastated by torrential rains and their homes were threatened by mud slides. One of the automobiles that came was a truck. This government vehicle was bringing people to discuss the damage with the villagers. The other car was also coming to help the villagers. There were 18 adults in our group and several teenagers with us. The teens and a few others, including myself, walked along a trail that led to the village. The rest of the adults piled into these two vehicles with our supplies and rode up to the village.

When we arrived, we were greeted by the beautiful indigenous families. We immediately got set up and started painting their school. The wonderful teenagers that were with us played soccer, jumped rope, and played other games with the children. They were so full of joy. It was lovely to watch them. When we finally took a lunch break, we played games with the children and watched them with total bliss as they experienced blowing bubbles for the first time! We also had fun playing hokey pokey with them. They loved it when we got to the part about turning ourselves around.

Now, for the other part of the miracle: the curvy, narrow, and treacherous dirt road. We were so grateful for fabulous weather. Had it rained, that dirt road would have been muddy, wet, and we wouldn't have been able to drive to the village. This was a tender mercy!

The next day the group went again to the village, where we helped rebuild a greenhouse that had been partially destroyed. The villagers' main food source was corn and potatoes. Someone from our group brought a few seeds to see if it was possible to help them grow other sources of nutrition. There were many homes close to the edge of the mountain, where mudslides threatened most. We saw government tents where some families were living temporarily until they could rebuild their homes because several of the homes had already slid off the side of the mountain. We were simply trying, in a small way, to help these beautiful people whose homes were being threatened.

Our efforts to help them in their trials blessed everyone with unexpected mercies.

Recently, I witnessed another wonderful tender mercy and miracle. I had received a text from my downstairs neighbor letting me know that water was coming from my condo upstairs. When I got home, I discovered that my air conditioning unit had a clogged PVC pipe and was leaking water into my neighbor's condo below. The last time I had someone address a problem with my AC, I felt like I had been taken advantage of and I believed they were dishonest. I immediately prayed that I would be guided on what to do. I called a dear friend, Jonathan, who works for an emergency clean up company. He was so kind and came right over. After a trip to Home Depot, he fixed part of the problem and brought over two professional, heavy-duty-24-hour fans that dry out floors and carpets that have been flooded. He also sprayed the wet areas so they wouldn't get moldy.

The next day, we realized that water was still leaking. I went to be by myself and specifically prayed out loud that Heavenly Father would send ministering angels to help me know who I should talk to, that they could diagnose the problem, fix it, and not break the bank for me. The next night Jonathan came over again and was frustrated because he knew there was a blockage, but couldn't find where it was. He told me I would need to call an AC specialist to fix the problem.

As the phone was in my hand to call the number of an AC specialist, a friend called. In the course of our conversation, I told her what was happening with my AC. She then said,

"Michelle, call Bill. That is what he does for a living." Bill was a mutual friend of ours from church. I called him, he came over within an hour, and diagnosed the problem in three minutes! Yes, three minutes! Within an hour and half, the problem was fixed and it cost me a total of $15 dollars in parts. What a tender mercy. I was so grateful for this wonderful miracle. God is truly in the details of our lives. He cares about us. As we draw upon the powers of heaven through prayer and call upon ministering angels, we will continue to see tender mercies in our lives.

The last story of tender mercy I want to share is not mine, but is that of an ecclesiastical leader named Ken and his lovely wife Kendra. They shared with me the blessings that occurred in their lives during the terminal illness of their son, Bryce. While Bryce was diagnosed with post-transplant lymphoproliferative disorder (PTLD) cancer, their family experienced many personal assurances in disguise that witnessed that God is truly in the details of our lives and in all circumstances.

After their son died at age 26, Ken and Kendra Moss made a list of 32 tender mercies that happened during his illness. With their permission, I will share a few of them:

- In 1985, after Bryce had his first kidney transplant and it failed, Ken was given three job opportunities which helped double their income (compensatory blessings) and helped pay for all their medical bills. This was a very stressful time!
- The Lord preserved Bryce's life in October and January. Bryce was not prepared to meet the Lord

then because he had a few unresolved things he needed to work out.

- The Lord blessed Bryce with Jerica (his girlfriend) and her family. Even though the last four months were some of the most difficult in terms of pain for Bryce, they were also the happiest.

- The Lord preserved Bryce's life for six weeks and allowed his parents the blessing of serving him, which they greatly cherish. They were able to be with him, and he was able to know someone was there, even when he was confused. His parents tried to help alleviate his pain, turn him to be comfortable, and help him brush his teeth. Kendra shared that she was able to sing to him and rub his feet and back to help calm him. Some told the family that Bryce could have passed away the first few days after he went into liver failure. While others with this disease have spend their last few weeks on a ventilator, Bryce rebounded and was off of a ventilator the last three weeks.

- Extended family members were able to help tend children. This allowed Bryce's sisters, Heidi and Alisha, to say good-bye to him in a timely manner.

- Bryce was purified with the refiners' fire during this difficult time, always expressing gratitude and a thumbs-up to everyone. He could even walk around the hospital after his coma—he was so determined to get better! The Lord was in the details of it all.

- Ken's work was close so he could take his computer and work at the hospital. His work allowed him to be very flexible.
- A miracle happened when Bryce turned 26. He was still covered under his parent's insurance until he passed, which helped tremendously financially. God intervened with this detail…in fact, God was in the details of all of it!
- Bryce's family grew closer through this adversity.
- Ken and Kendra received many kindnesses from numerous friends and family.
- Many meals and visits were given to their family. Ken was serving as a local clergy man at the time, and Ken had many demands of his time.

Ken and Kendra both received the gift of greater empathy for others because of their suffering. During this arduous time, they were able to see God in the details and the tender mercies in disguise. I have been strengthened by this couple's faith through such a difficult experience and their ability to see the Lord's hand amidst adversity!

Think of a difficult time in your life. I know it can be hard to go there emotionally. Think back, and if you look with God's understanding and teaching, you will see there were miracles along the way. I challenge you to remember the tender mercies and miracles in life even when, *and especially when,* life is hard. WRITE THEM DOWN! Also, I challenge you to believe that *compensatory blessings will come.* The

Trials Can Be Mercies in Disguise

Lord will compensate us for all of our sufferings and trials in this life.

In the last example shared, this family was experiencing 'long suffering' as they watched their son pass beyond the veil into the heavens. Seeing God's mercy in their lives, while they waited through this time and served Bryce, is a perfect example of *being angels while we wait in life!* I love and appreciate the example of Ken and Kendra Moss.

> "God gives us hope because he gives us himself.
> He wants us to know we are never alone."
> (Max Lucado)[9]

CHAPTER 8

Defy Your Limits

"See your dreams come to pass. You must conceive it and believe it is possible if you ever hope to experience it. To conceive it, you must have an image on the inside of the life you want to live on the outside. The image has to become a part of you, in your thoughts, your conversation, deep down in your subconscious mind, in your actions, in every part of your being."
Joel Osteen[10]

While *waiting between now and when in life*, I like to challenge myself in positive ways. I love how Joel Osteen challenges us in his book *Live Your Best Life Now* to 'enlarge your vision'. I want to grow spiritually, mentally, physically, in all ways that I can to be what the Lord needs me to be. In January 2016, I made my typical New Year's goals; one of which was to hike Mount Timpanogos in Utah. After starting out the year with a miserable case of pneumonia, I wondered how the rest of my year would turn out.

Defy Your Limits

I started hiking every Wednesday and Saturday in May of that year in preparation for my goal and was grateful for a couple of wonderful friends who hiked with me. The week of the Mount Timpanogos hike, I prayed that I would have ministering angels, and my family members that had passed on, to help me up to the summit. On the day of the hike, we left our homes at 3:40 a.m. to hit the trail just after 4:10 a.m. We realized at over a mile and a half into the hike that we were on the wrong trail. I started to feel discouraged and didn't know if I could hike 16 miles plus 3.7 more miles that day. We headed back to the parking lot so we could take the right trail. As my mental state was a little gloomy, I heard the thought clearly in my head, *"I survived Vietnam, you can do this."* I knew it was my Uncle Roger who had passed away four years earlier from lung cancer. I felt strengthened and knew I would have help that day.

While hiking, we saw more than two dozen mountain goats, beautiful wildflowers, majestic mountain peaks, lush landscapes, and bright blue skies. I knew God had created all of this for us to truly enjoy in our lives!

It was an extremely strenuous hike! When we finally reached the saddle, the view was breathtaking—we could see for miles and miles in all directions. It was a beautiful clear day. I really must admit, I was worn-out and didn't know if I could go another step. The summit was one more mile up a steep, narrow, and rocky terrain. One of my best friends, Camille Kennard, was with me. She was such an amazing cheerleader all along the way. She kept saying, "You can do hard things; you've got this!" Her dad helped me through all the really steep areas, and I was grateful for their love and support! ☺

The last few stretches to the summit, I struggled with nausea from altitude sickness. Finally, I made it to the top and saw the most magnificent, stunning view! I felt such a deep

sense of accomplishment. We had a rough start, but we did it! I ran out of water with 5 miles left before we reached the trailhead, and the last 4-5 miles were the worst miles of my life. My feet ached so badly, I almost cried when I finally reached the parking lot. I had truly pushed beyond my physical limits. Camille, who is a social worker and life coach, has a sign on her vision board, showing her goals. It says, *"Live to defy your limits."* She helped me achieve that goal for myself.

On a trip to the Polochic Valley in Guatemala, I did basic oral hygiene education and provided local anesthesia for villagers needing to see the dentist for abscessed teeth. Many of their teeth needed extracting, had infections, or were rotted out (sadly, there were many). Each day we set up a clinic in a different village, driving from village to village in the back of a cattle car. One particular day, many of our medical and dental staff were struggling with traveler's diarrhea. We were low on staff and should have called it a day, but there were so many people waiting to see us that we decided to stay and see as many as we could.

In the remote area where we were serving, there were two different languages spoken, Spanish and Q'eqchi. We needed two translators, one to translate English to Spanish and one to translate from Spanish to Q'eqchi. I personally never met someone that was fluent in all three. We also had no electricity or running water. We had to bring in bottled water to use for sterilization. There were more than 30 families waiting outside to be seen for dental care alone.

Our other hygienist was helping in another village that day, so I was by myself screening and triaging. A young father of four came in with a significant abscess and some swelling in his face. This was NOT a good sign, and we were not in a position to give him optimal care with certain antibiotics. Consequently, I numbed him on the side of his face where the infection was, which provided immediate relief, and walked over to our medical clinic to see if they had a stronger antibiotic to give him.

On my way there, several mothers grabbed at me asking with their facial expressions for me to "please see their children." One lady was pointing at her 3-year-old, signaling for me to look in her mouth. Meanwhile, she had an infant on her hip who had something moving under the skin of its eyelid. I gently clasped her hand and signaled for her to follow me. She kept putting my hands toward her 3-year-old. When I got to the medical clinic (which also had a long line), I asked if they had a stronger antibiotic and the attending nurse gave me a 'what the heck is that?' look about the infant's eye. We found out later that the child had a parasite under its eyelid.

Eventually, I started to make my way back to the dental clinic. While walking back, I could tell by the expressions on the faces of many of the mothers that they were begging for help for their children. It was overwhelming. On top of it all, that day, we had an English/Spanish translator, but we did not have a translator that spoke Spanish and Q'eqchi, which was vital to communicate to the young father how to take his antibiotic regimen.

I couldn't take the stress anymore! I told my friend Adam, who was holding a flashlight for me to see while I was administering local anesthesia, "I need just a minute." I went into a corner in the dark (again, we had no running water or electricity and very limited provisions). There was nowhere else to go, as many families were right outside the door or near the one window that we had. I couldn't hold back the tears and started to cry. Then I prayed, "Heavenly Father, this is too much. I am in way over my head here. I don't speak their language. I don't even know this man's name. Please help him understand that he needs to take this medicine everyday like he's supposed to. Please, Father help me!" I had a quick breakdown of tears and suddenly I felt super calm, and with a clear mind thought, *Michelle, you are more than enough. I know you don't know this language or his name, but I DO. Go back over there, (I was literally two feet away from the crowd) I know Q'eqchi and I know each of these people by name. I've got this and I've got you!* I then

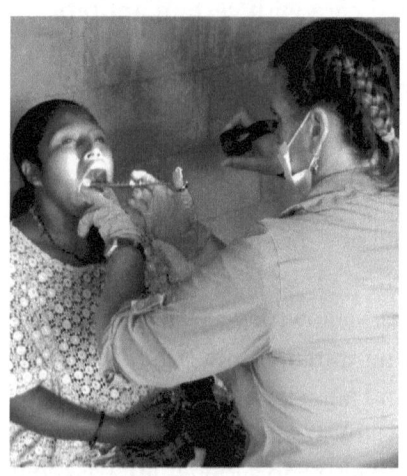

squared my shoulders, took a deep breath, turned around and said, "Okay, I am ready." Adam, who was helping me, said, "What just happened?" I said, "I'll tell you later." He said he could tell by my face something had happened. About five minutes later, a villager walked in and asked if we needed a translator who spoke Q'eqchi. He spoke this language along with Spanish and ended up translating for us and telling the young father all that he needed to do for the post treatment of his extraction.

We experienced a truly tender mercy and miracle! I will always be grateful for Heavenly Father's friendly reminder to me that *He knows ALL of us by name and is aware of ALL our needs.* We can do hard things with His help!

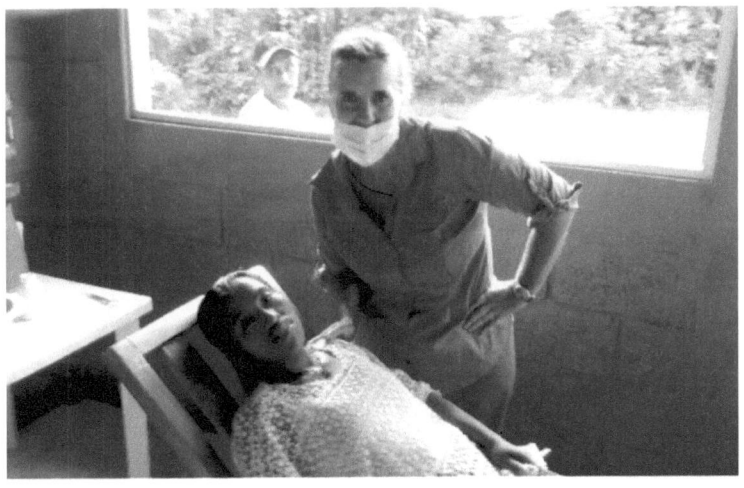

When life gets hard and the *waiting* is excruciating—challenge yourself! Whether you take a spiritual challenge like reading the entire *Bible* in one year, or you want to learn a new language, take an art or Tai Chi class, or hike a mountain—push yourself! You can do hard things. Enlarge your vision and see no limits. Ask for ministering angels to help you. *Live to defy your limits!*

CHAPTER 9

Sling and a Stone

"...David prevailed over the Philistine with a sling and with a stone, and smote the Philistine, and slew him..."
(1 Samuel 17:50)

One of the great stories of courage from the *Old Testament* is the description of David's encounter with Goliath. There are many applications we can use in our own lives, and it is an account I need to read more often! This story is found in 1 Samuel 17. First, we discover that Goliath of Gath (the Giant) is six cubits and a span in height. After doing a little research, I found that this measurement indicates that Goliath was 9 feet 9-inches tall. To me, facing a 9-foot 9-inch-tall giant would have been very intimidating, but not for David. He was full of courage and faith. He took a moment to remember the Lord's help and deliverance in earlier circumstances. This is a great message to us when we are full of doubt, fear, or despair.

We all, at one time or another, will face our Goliaths. Think about your life—what is yours? Is it a defiant child or a wayward spouse? Is it a marriage that is distant and falling apart? Is it some form of addiction? Is it pornography, time in front of the computer with social media, or prescription drugs? Is it unemployment or being under-employed? Is it singlehood, loneliness, or an unexpected tragedy in your family? Is it death, divorce, depression, illness, or infertility? Is it time management and finding balance? The list of possibilities goes on and on, but everyone has their own Goliaths.

So how can David's example help us as we face our own Goliaths in life? We read in 1 Samuel 17:37: "David said, moreover, The Lord that delivered me out of the paw of the lion, and out of the paw of the bear, he will deliver me out of the hand of this Philistine. And Saul said unto David, Go, and the Lord be with thee."

Again, we read how David remembered the Lord's hand and deliverance. This is a friendly reminder to me that as we have difficult things in front of us we need to *remember* earlier times when the Lord has helped us, delivered us, or given us miracles. We've all had them! We must *remember* that if He helped us through a hard time before, He will help us through a hard time now. The day of miracles has NOT ceased! As we continue, we read the whole incident of David against the Philistine Goliath:

> And when the Philistine looked about, and saw David, he disdained him: for he was but a youth, and ruddy, and of a fair countenance. *(Do we have times*

when others may scorn us, bully us, look down on us, or tell us we don't measure up?)

And the Philistine said unto David, Am I a dog, that thou comest to me with staves? And the Philistine cursed David by his gods.

And the Philistine said to David, Come to me, and I will give thy flesh unto the fowls of the air, and to the beasts of the field. *(Sounds similar to some modern day bullying.)*

Then said David to the Philistine, Thou comest to me with a sword, and with a spear, and with a shield: but I come to thee in the name of the Lord of hosts, the God of the armies of Israel, whom thou hast defied.

This day will the Lord deliver thee into mine hand; and I will smite thee, and take thine head from thee; and I will give the carcasses of the host of the Philistines this day unto the fowls of the air, and to the wild beasts of the earth; that all the earth may know that there is a God in Israel. *(Remember he is looking at a giant that is 9 feet 9-inches-tall standing in front of him.* ☺*)*

And all this assembly shall know that the Lord saveth not with sword and spear: for the battle is the Lord's, and he will give you into our hands.

And it came to pass, when the Philistine arose, and came and drew nigh to meet David, that David hasted, and ran toward the army to meet the Philistine.

And David put his hand in his bag, and took thence a stone, and slang it, and smote the Philistine

> in his forehead, that the stone sunk into his forehead; and he fell upon his face to the earth. *(Just an interesting side note: we read earlier in verse 40 that he chose five stones and had them with him in his bag. He only needed one, nonetheless, he was prepared for whatever he needed to do.)*
> So David prevailed over the Philistine with a sling and with a stone, and smote the Philistine, and slew him; but there was no sword in the hand of David.
> Therefore David ran, and stood upon the Philistine, and took his sword, and drew it out of the sheath thereof, and slew him, and cut off his head therewith. And when the Philistines saw their champion was dead, they fled. (1 Samuel 17:42-51)

I would like to share with you one of the Goliaths in life that I have had to face. Now, before I start, I want to make it clear that I believe I am truly blessed with a good life. With that said, I will share with you that one of the biggest challenges and questions that I don't have an answer for is my experience of 'waiting to marry' and share my life with someone. For a very long time, I listened to Satan's lies telling me it was because I did something wrong, or wasn't pretty enough, or missed an opportunity somewhere. Year after year, I have watched more friends marry, have children, and now they are sending their kids to college. Of course, I am so happy for my friends when the great events of life (marriage, children, grandchildren, etc.) happen for them. I must admit though, that it is hard to understand why the Lord hasn't seen to provide me with this blessing.

Sling and a Stone

Yet, in the last few years, I have come to understand that God does love me. He knows me and He truly wants the best for me. I used to jokingly say that I'm working on Plan B, then Plan C, and eventually I got to Plan S. However, *I now know* that I am living the Lord's Plan A for me. Just because these blessings haven't been realized doesn't mean that He loves me less or wants less for me! It just means that His plan and purpose for my life is different than I expected. I can choose to doubt and despair (trust me I have, it's not fun), or I can choose, as David did, to remember the Lord's hand in my life in earlier times and know that He is here for me now.

Having lost both of my parents, I also struggle with wanting to belong to a family with whom I can share my life. I have a brother and sister in the Portland, Oregon area who I love very much, but we don't live close to each other. This can make holidays very lonely. I have been blessed with great friends, but I long for a family of my own. Most of the time, I feel at peace and live a very purposeful and abundant life. However, there are moments, usually holidays, that can cut so deep to the core of my heart that I think it could literally bleed. I want to sanctify *this waiting time* to God's purposes and helping others!

Back to David, he had in his pocket five smooth stones, but only used one. He put them in his shepherd's bag and had his sling in hand. This was how he prepared himself to face the Philistine, Goliath. What are the stones and slings in our lives? These are the measure of our life preparations. Although there are many to prepare, I'd like to share five smooth stones, and the one sling of my own, that have truly blessed my life.

First Stone—Gratitude

It takes effort to exercise gratitude and have an optimistic approach to life. Yet the Lord truly blesses us, and His tender mercies should not go unnoticed or unappreciated.

One challenge I'd like to suggest is something I learned from my mother. My amazing mother always had thank you cards on hand. She sent many thank you notes and Christmas cards. I believe correspondence of gratitude expands the soul. I know for myself, when I unexpectedly receive a letter of appreciation it warms my heart. Years ago, I decided to keep a box of notes at work and in my church tote bag. I've had many opportunities to speak professionally and teach at church, so I know preparation can take a lot of effort. This has helped me to be more aware of people's commitments and express appreciation for the little things they do. I know I could still improve at this, and I want to work at cultivating my attribute of gratitude.

> "Sing unto the Lord, O ye saints of his, and give thanks at the remembrance of his holiness."
> (Psalms 30:4)

As we live close to Jesus and His teachings, we will be enriched and strengthened. In the beautiful book *The Hiding Place*, Corrie ten Boom shares her experience while living with her sister Betsie in a German concentration camp. Betsie chose to have an attitude of gratitude in the bleakest conditions (there is something to be said about learning from someone else's trials, during their own furnaces of affliction). In Corrie ten Boom's personal account of the experience, she describes how she and her sister miraculously smuggled a *Bible* into their living quarters. One night as the two sisters sat up reading the *New Testament,* they came across a scripture that spoke of giving thanks in all things. Betsie and Corrie lived in a building that held 1,400 prisoners even though it was designed to hold only 400. Nine people shared their bunk for four. When fleas infested their small area and the building's toilets overflowed, Betsie chose to express gratitude. She saw a miracle in the fact that she and Corrie were located in the same camp and sleeping in the same bunk, and that because of the fleas, the guards left her and her sister alone.[11] Corrie ten Boom describes a conversation with Betsie as follows:

> "That's it, Corrie! That's His answer. 'Give thanks in all things, in all circumstances!' That's what we can do. We can start right now to thank God for every single thing about this new barracks!"
> I stared at her, then around me at the dark, foul-aired room.
> "Such as?" I said.
> "Such as being assigned here together."
> I bit my lip. "Oh yes, Lord Jesus."
> "Such as what you are holding in your hands."
> "I looked down at the *Bible.* "Yes! Thank You, dear Lord, that there was no inspection when we entered here! Thank You for all of the women, here in this room, who will meet You in these pages."
> "Yes," said Betsie. "Thank You for the very crowding in here, since we are packed so close; that

many more will hear!…Thank You," Betsie went on serenely, "for the fleas and for—

The fleas! This was too much. "Betsie, there's no way even God can make me grateful for a flea."

"Give thanks in all circumstances," she quoted.

"It doesn't say, 'in pleasant circumstances.' Fleas are part of this place where God has put us."[12]

Later in the book, the reader learns that many other women in this concentration camp were beaten and raped during their stay there. But because of the infestation of the fleas, the guards did not touch Betsie and Corrie. (If that were my story, I would call it *The Miracle of the Fleas!*) Betsie's gratitude made me stop and think. In gloomy circumstances, I sometimes tend to whine and complain instead of having Betsie's attitude.

From time to time, I'm guilty of murmuring and refusing to see the bigger picture. After my father passed away, I felt overwhelmed with grief and still mourned the loss of my mother. I remember a moment when even though I was sad, I knew that God lived and that His saving grace and redemption power was real. In that moment, I chose to believe, chose to hope, chose to know God still had a plan for me. And I chose to move forward. Of course, I still mourned and grieved; however, I strongly felt the peace that surpasses all understanding.

Second Stone—Personal Prayer

We are never beyond the reach of our Heavenly Father, and we are always in need of cultivating a relationship with Him.

Sling and a Stone

One day while doing inner city missionary service in Decatur, Illinois, my friend and I came upon a lady who was really struggling. She lived in a neighborhood that was full of crime, drugs, and dangerous conditions. As we walked through the neighborhood, we saw a woman who appeared to be several months pregnant, sitting in a rocking chair on the porch of an old, run-down house. She held a cigarette, and we watched her take a few puffs from it. Two toddlers darted around a front yard overgrown with tall grass and weeds. We decided to find out about this woman and her story. We walked up the cracked concrete driveway and introduced ourselves to the woman. She said her name was Cheryl and that she was twenty-seven years old. She had five or six children, each with a different father, and the father of the child she would soon give birth to was in prison for drug use. After we talked with Cheryl for a long time, she disclosed that she had been sexually abused as a child. Tragically, it was a religious leader, a pastor, that abused her. Consequently, Cheryl had some reservations about discussing religion. She also admitted that she didn't know how to read. We spent the rest of the afternoon talking with Cheryl about prayer and telling her that we knew Heavenly Father loved her and cared about her life.

While we were visiting with Cheryl, a friend of hers named Vicki dropped by. Vicki had been staying in a woman's shelter because she had been a victim of domestic violence. She had left her baby with Cheryl overnight while she stayed at the shelter, and she said that the baby was inside Cheryl's house. We'd been talking for a long time on the porch, so we decided to go in and see if the baby was okay, guessing that Cheryl had been sitting on the porch all day, leaving the baby unattended. As we entered the house, there were no lights on, just sunlight slivering through the curtain windows. We saw cockroaches climbing all over the walls and floor. I walked across the room and started to smell the horrible stench of urine. As I approached the baby, the smell got stronger. The baby whimpered softly, but it stopped crying as I picked him up. His clothing was soaked with urine, so I took him into the bathroom, and as I turned on the light, cockroaches scattered everywhere. I took the diaper off the baby and it looked as though something like mold had formed in the diaper. As I turned on the water to try to bathe the baby, a horde of cockroaches came out of the pipes.

After we tried to care for the baby, we talked with Cheryl and Vicki again, asking if we could teach them how to pray. Cheryl said she wasn't sure if there was a God, but if there was, He didn't love her because of all she had done in her life and because of what happened to her when she was a little girl. We told Cheryl to just pretend there is a God, to just pretend He is there, and just pretend He will answer. We taught Cheryl the basic steps of prayer, and she agreed to try to pray. The four of us knelt in her living room after pulling the drapes to let in some light. Cheryl started, "Heavenly Father, are you there?" Immediately, we all felt the Spirit strongly, even with cockroaches crawling all over us. Cheryl went on, "Do you love me even though I haven't lived the best life?" We could all feel the power of God's love in that room and I don't know if I've felt it more strongly since. It was amazing. All four of us had tears in our eyes as the Spirit bore witness of God's love for Cheryl.

For the next two weeks, we visited with Cheryl for an hour a day. We read about Jesus Christ from the scriptures, we washed

Sling and a Stone

and cut her children's hair and, we cleaned her house. We found weevils in the baby bottles, and so we boiled them. Because of some other obligations, we went a few days without seeing her and the children. We kept feeling that we should go see Cheryl, but we just didn't make it. On a Monday, we walked to Cheryl's house and found an official-looking note on the door that said, "UNFIT FOR HUMAN OCCUPANCY." A neighbor told us that Child Protective Services had come and taken the children and condemned the house. We never found out where Cheryl went, and we never saw her again. Nevertheless, I'm so grateful that we had the opportunity to serve her, and teach her that she was a child of the Most High God and that He loved her—and that we were able to teach her how to pray.

As mentioned before, John McCain was a prisoner of war in Vietnam and suffered many brutal beatings. He later wrote this about prayer, "I was finding that prayer helped. It wasn't a question of asking for superhuman strength or for God to strike the North Vietnamese dead. It was asking for moral and physical courage, for guidance and wisdom to do the right thing. I asked for comfort when I was in pain, and sometimes I received relief. I was sustained in many times of trial."

A while back, I was challenged to keep a prayer journal. It has been a very powerful blessing in my life! I am so easily distracted that I sometimes find myself thinking of my "to do" list while I am praying. I think about if I took the garbage out, shut the window, or if I called that person at work. Sometimes I start to think of different conversations throughout the day. My thoughts go on and on. It is very distracting and it limits me from really feeling the Spirit of the Lord and focusing on what He would have me learn from Him.

Writing it down, articulating a prayer on paper like a letter to our Heavenly Father and King, where I can pour out my concerns, express gratitude, and share other things on my mind, helps me focus. I read scriptures for a few minutes and listen to some uplifting music to help set the tone and invite the Spirit. Then I turn the page in my journal and continue to say a silent prayer for Heavenly Father's answer, putting pen on the paper and listening to the revelation and inspiration that comes. The process has been extremely powerful and such a beautiful experience as I receive God's truths pertaining to my life and how He feels about me.

Recently I traveled to Chicago for work. Before I left, I offered a prayer, like I usually do in the morning. This time, however, I asked for ministering angels to watch over me and protect me from my house all the way to the hotel door. I made it to the airport, flew to Chicago, and took the train into town. My hotel was only four blocks from my stop. When I got off the train, I was looking at the Google Map app on my phone to figure out which way to go. A man approached me and asked if he could help me find my way. I felt I should be cautious. He followed me all the way to my hotel. When we were halfway there, I thanked him for his kindness and said I could make it from there (of course, in a nice-toned voice). He started yelling at me on the street, telling me I was a racist, that I didn't belong in Chicago, and a few other colorful things. I started to panic a little. Then, I remembered my prayer. I had prayed for ministering angels to watch over me all the way to the hotel door. I knew I wasn't alone! I kept walking to the hotel, and the man followed me. When we got to the hotel he asked me for money for taking me there. He said I could go to an ATM machine to pay him. I quickly went indoors and after checking into my room (a bit freaked out) I said a prayer of thanks for the ministering angels that watched over me and kept me safe. I am grateful for prayer!

Take the time to pray vocally as often as possible, and on your knees if you can. Be specific in both your gratitude and your petitions. As you do this, your love for Heavenly Father and His son Jesus Christ will increase, and you will learn how much They love you! It is only through prayer that you can truly learn more of your purposes here on earth. You have many things to accomplish, and many blessings await you if you just ask for them.

Third Stone—Repent, and Receive God's Amazing Grace

A powerful example of the Lord's forgiveness and grace is found in the story of John Newton. Newton was a slave trader in the mid-1700s. On his watch, over twenty thousand African slaves—men, women, and children—died due to the inhumane conditions on the ships that transported them to America. One night in March 1748, Newton's ship *The Greyhound* almost sank during a furious Atlantic storm. As the storm raged, Newton realized the enormity of his sins and pleaded for God to forgive him, promising that if God spared his life, he would spend it trying to make amends for his wrongdoings. Keeping his promise, Newton devoted his life to the ministry and to working for the abolition of slavery. He was a mentor to Wilbur Wilberforce, a member of the British Parliament whose efforts contributed to the abolishment of the slave trade throughout the British Empire. John Newton never ceased to stand in awe of God's work in his life. His is a great story of a man's triumph over demons, of true repentance, and of making retribution for one's sins.[13] It was Newton who wrote the words to one of our most beloved hymns, *Amazing Grace*. "Amazing Grace, how sweet the sound that saved a wretch like me. I once was lost, but now I'm found, was blind, but now I see!"

In March 1805, the elderly John Newton wrote in his diary, "Not well able to write, but I endeavor to observe the return of this day with humiliation, prayer and praise. Only God's amazing grace could and would take a rude, profane, slave trading sailor and transform him into a child of God."[14]

> "For by grace are ye saved through faith;
> and that not of yourselves: it is the gift of God:
> Not of works, lest any man should boast."
> (Ephesians 2:8-9)

Fourth Stone—Service to Others

Service to others brings us closer to the Lord's Spirit. One of the great blessings of my job is being around colleagues and associates in the community that give so much of their time and compassion to helping others. I work with many dental hygienists who volunteer an abundant amount of time to helping under-served populations. I also work with other health professionals, dentists, pediatricians, physician assistants, and others that significantly give of their time and skills to bless the lives of others. They are endowed with goodness as they give back to the community they live in. They might not know it, but I believe they are *armed with spiritual life slings*. ☺

Sling and a Stone

One of my favorite responsibilities of my job (frankly, a sacred privilege), is overseeing the dental screenings during the Healthy Athletes Clinic at the Fall and Summer Special Olympics. Nothing warms my heart more than seeing these athletes come in with their medals on. I love to work with dental hygiene students as well as dental students, overseeing their volunteer work at these events.

While in Orlando, Florida at a training for the Special Olympics, specifically for Clinic Directors, I experienced a tender mercy. Our group was running dental screenings and in the midst of screening hundreds of athletes, I had a very clear impression that God knew and loved all the athletes I was screening. They were so innocent and pure. It is such a sacred privilege to work with athletes who have special healthcare needs. I feel very strongly that dental students and dental hygiene students should work with this wonderful population while in school because they will likely see them in their practices when they get out of school. At the beginning of each shift, some of the student volunteers are nervous to do dental screenings on adults and children with intellectual disabilities, as it can sometimes be challenging work. However, by the end of their shifts, they are high-fiving and hugging the athletes, and smiling and congratulating them on their races. It is priceless to see this change in just a few hours.

One of my regular clinical volunteers (and now Co-Clinical Dental Director of the Special Smiles Dental Screenings at the Special Olympics) is Kathy Harris. She is a dental hygienist and such an example of selfless service. Kathy jumps in to help whenever we've been in a pinch. One time when I had a dental screener cancel at the last minute, Kathy dropped what she was doing and came in an instant. She was there early, stayed late, and helped me out tremendously. The athletes love her! 😊

There are several other services provided for the athletes such as vision tests, podiatrist evaluations, wellness checkups, and hearing checks. Each of these different clinics have up to 35 volunteers helping over a two-day period. All the volunteers come on their own time and dime and love working with the athletes. If you want to be armed with God's love and power, serve those who can't otherwise help themselves. It is so powerful! I'm always impressed with the selfless service that so many of our volunteers render.

Frequently in my job, I provide oral health education and preventative care to Migrant Head Starts, Native Americans, Long Term Care Facilities, Refugee Health Fairs, and so many more collaborations and events. I have seen volunteer after volunteer, who come from all walks of life, donate their time to give back to the communities they live in. It is such a sacred privilege to witness this weekly in my life.

Fifth Stone—Offer Forgiveness

The summer between my junior and senior years in high school, my dear friend Lisa experienced a terrible tragedy in her family. Her father, a psychiatrist, was shot and killed in his office by one of his male patients. Understandably, this was an extremely difficult time for Lisa and her family. A few years after high school, Lisa mentioned that she needed to forgive her father's murderer so that she could move forward in life. Lisa later became a nurse and understood more about mental illness and what her father had dedicated his life to; helping the mentally ill become functioning members of society. He helped thousands. Lisa never got complete closure with her father's death, so it has been important for her to keep the lines of communication open with her husband, children, and other family members and friends. She doesn't like to leave anything unresolved, even just overnight, and she never wants to live with the regret of having unfinished words with a loved one. Lisa possesses a healthy sense of self and has triumphed over a terrible tragedy.

 When I spoke with her recently, Lisa said that hating her father's murderer, or holding a grudge against him, was a waste of energy. She explained that it was a choice to forgive. Obviously, such understanding didn't come to Lisa overnight, the deepest insights never do. But I am grateful for her powerful example. In the face of adversity, Lisa chose to move forward and focus on the good things in her life. Our Father in Heaven pleads with us to approach Him with a repentant heart and an attitude of forgiveness toward others. As we let go of anger and learn to forgive others, we open ourselves to love in our life. Lisa is a great example of forgiveness in extremely difficult circumstances. As an opposite example, an acquaintance of mine hasn't spoken to her mother for almost twenty years. While I don't know the circumstances, and don't seek to judge her or her mother, the situation seems tragic, no matter the reasons for the silence. Until we forgive those who have hurt us, we carry festering wounds in our soul that prevent us from truly being whole in other relationships. That said, in situations where there have been severe offenses, a person may need professional counseling to help process difficult emotions and to move toward forgiveness and peace. From the Redeemer of the world, we learn the greatest lesson of forgiveness. On the cross, He said, "Father, forgive them for they know not what they do." (Luke 23:34)

One last striking example of forgiveness comes again from the life of Corrie ten Boom. After the war ended, this Holocaust survivor shared with groups of all faiths her testimony of the Savior's peace and of the miracle of repentance. Here is her amazing account of one such experience:

> "It was at a church service in Munich that I saw him, the former S.S. man who had stood guard at the shower room door in the processing center at Ravensbruck. He was the first of our actual jailers that I had seen since that time. And suddenly it was all there—the roomful of mocking men, the heaps of clothing, Betsie's pain-blanched face.
>
> He came up to me as the church was emptying, beaming and bowing. "How grateful I am for your message, Fraulein," he said. "To think that, as you say, He has washed my sins away!" His hand was thrust out to shake mine. And I, who had preached so often to the people in Bloemendaal the need to forgive, kept my hand at my side.
>
> Even as the angry, vengeful thoughts boiled through me, I saw the sin of them. Jesus Christ had died for this man; was I going to ask for more? Lord Jesus, I prayed, forgive me and help me to forgive him.
>
> I tried to smile; I struggled to raise my hand. I could not. I felt nothing, not the slightest spark of warmth or charity. And so again I breathed a silent prayer. Jesus, I cannot forgive him. Give me Your forgiveness.

Sling and a Stone

As I took his hand the most incredible thing happened. From my shoulder along my arm and through my hand a current seemed to pass from me to him, while into my heart sprang a love for this stranger that almost overwhelmed me.

And so I discovered that it is not on our forgiving any more than on our goodness that the world's healing hinges, but on His. When He tells us to love our enemies, He gives along with the command, the love itself."[15]

One Sling—Surround Yourself with Positive People

Although David needed only the one stone to conquer Goliath, he was prepared with both the five stones and his sling. I've shared what my five stones are. Now, I'd like to share a sling that is important in my life. Without it I wouldn't be able to use my five stones as effectively.

Although there have been many 'spiritual' slings that have helped me in my life, there is one that has truly affected the course of my life, *to surround myself with uplifting people!* This has been an invaluable and effective offensive approach, a proactive way of building my spiritual and emotional support team. The image on the following page is a photo of some of my life-long best friends from my home state of Oregon. They are angels in my life, wonderful uplifting friends the Lord has blessed me with. ☺

This sling has also helped me stay in check to be a person who is uplifting to others. Are there people in your life that put others down? Are there people in your life that are toxic? People who are always complaining about life? People who

Between the Now and When

are like Eeyore, who are always moping about how bad life is? Maybe someone who uses bad language or talks about others behind their back? Do you have friends or family that attend worship services? That serve others? Are kind to others? Listen without judgment? Think about who is in your life—do they bring you closer to Christ, or invite toxic energy into your life?

I'm grateful for David's wonderful example of how he conquered Goliath. Let us ascend and upgrade our life to be ready to face our modern-day Goliaths armed with God's power! I have experienced for myself, that as we live with gratitude, increase the meaningfulness of our personal prayers, repent more, ask for forgiveness, and take opportunities to serve others, we can conquer today's Goliaths!

A final challenge I give to each of us is to pray to know how best to dedicate this time *between now and when* in life. Pray to have the Lord expand our vision of how best we can spend our *waiting times* in life. Don't compare yourself to what others are doing. Whatever your limits are, God will reach your reaching. God knows YOU by name and speaks your name often! The Spirit is a beautiful companion and a gift that we can call upon to guide and direct us. BELIEVE THIS. May we have the courage to be all HE wants and needs us to be, and to find joy in living an abundant life! ☺

These are more angels in my life!

Questions for a Book Club Discussion

- Share something that has been a challenge in your life when you have been in a 'holding pattern.' How have you felt the Lord's help through this time? What actions have you taken or can take to help you? ☺

- Share with each other one or two angels in your life who have truly helped you. (This might be your parents, siblings, friends, even a stranger, etc.). ☺

- Is there a time in your life that you were able to declare God's love to others? If so, please share. Or, on the flip side, is there a time in your life when someone helped you see God's love for you? Please share. ☺

- How can we better love our neighbors? ☺

- Is there someone you know serving in the military or who has in the past? If so, share with the group information about this person—on an individual level. Write to this person a letter expressing gratitude for his/her service. If there is a family that you know whose loved one is currently serving abroad, take them some cookies, or offer to help with the kids or cleaning. Follow in the Savior's footsteps of service! Or, as a group, go provide service for this family. ☺

- Write down a future goal and share it with each other. Write it on a sticky note or some paper where you will visually see this goal everyday (bathroom mirror, fridge, etc.). Share how you can support one another to attain your goals, or how you can defy limits to achieve your goals. Your goal can be anything: hike a mountain, read the *Bible* in six months, take a cooking class, express gratitude in your prayers every day, interview a grandparent about his/her past, walk every day for 30 minutes, the list goes on. The point is, to choose something and know that God will help you reach and surpass your goals. He can help us *defy our limits!* ☺

Notes

1. Joel Osteen, Your Best Life Now, Faith Words, 2004, 231
2. Paraphrased from the hymn http://www.hymntime.com/tch/htm/l/o/v/loveofgo.htm
3. Neal A. Maxwell, All These Things Shall Give Thee Experience, Salt Lake City, Deseret Book, 1980, 46
4. Dale Carnegie, How to Win Friends and Influence People, Pocket Books, 1981
5. Ezra T. Benson, "The Constitution—A Heavenly Banner," BYU Devotional Talk, September 16, 1986
6. Billygraham.org
7. USCCB.org
8. Max Lucado, God Will Carry You, Thomas Nelson, Inc, 2013, 62
9. Max Lucado, God Will Carry You, Thomas Nelson, Inc, 2013, 176
10. Joel Osteen, Your Best Life Now, Faith Words, 2004, 4
11. Corrie ten Boom with Elizabeth Sherril and John Sherril, The Hiding Place, Old Tappan, NJ: Fleming H. Revell Co., 1971, 198–99
12. Corrie ten Boom with Elizabeth Sherril and John Sherril, The Hiding Place, Old Tappan, NJ: Fleming H. Revell Co., 1971, 198–99

13. Jonathan Aitken, John Newton: From Disgrace to Amazing Grace (Wheaton, IL: Crossway Books Publishing, 2007), quoted in documentary: How Sweet the Sound: The Story of Amazing Grace, by William Christie
14. Al Rogers, Amazing Grace: The Story of John Newton, www.reformedreader.org, originally published in an issue of "Away Here in Texas," July–Aug., 1996
15. Corrie ten Boom with Elizabeth Sherril and John Sherril, The Hiding Place, Old Tappan, NJ: Fleming H. Revell Co., 1971, 238

About the Author

Michelle L. Martin was raised in Portland, Oregon. She received a Bachelor's Degree in Dental Hygiene from Weber State University, and a Master's Degree in Public Health from the University of Utah. Currently, Michelle works at the Utah Department of Health as the Oral Health Specialist for the state of Utah. She works with vulnerable populations and helps them access dental care. She is also the Utah Dental Hygiene Liaison for the National Center on Early Childhood Health and Wellness (NCECHW). She serves as a communication link between NCECHW and Head Start, state, territory, and tribal childcare agencies on topics related to improving the oral health of pregnant women and children enrolled in Head Start and childcare. Her passion for working with staff and families enrolled in Head Start led her to develop innovative oral health initiatives in tribal and migrant communities. She is also the Co-Dental Director for Healthy Smiles with the Utah Special Olympics, overseeing dental screenings and referrals. One of Michelle's loves in life has been traveling abroad on humanitarian trips to provide oral hygiene and dental care. She has been to the Marshall Islands, Vietnam, Peru, Guatemala, and Honduras.